REINVENTING LIFELONG LEARNING

VITAL INFORMATION FOR EDUCATORS AND POLICYMAKERS

REINVENTING LIFELONG LEARNING

The Coming Renaissance Of Continuing Education And Community Outreach

EDWARD LOUIS ABEYTA, PHD

REINVENTING LIFELONG LEARNING
The Coming Renaissance
Of Continuing Education
And Community Outreach

© 2024 by Edward L. Abeyta

All rights reserved.

Printed in the United States of America.

No part of this publication may be reproduced or distributed in any form or by any means, without the prior permission of the publisher. Requests for permission should be directed to permissions@indiebooksintl.com, or mailed to Permissions, Indie Books International, 2511 Woodlands Way, Oceanside, CA 92054.

The views and opinions in this book are those of the author at the time of writing this book, and do not reflect the opinions of Indie Books International or its editors.

Neither the publisher nor the author is engaged in rendering legal or other professional services through this book. If expert assistance is required, the services of appropriate professionals should be sought. The publisher and the author shall have neither liability nor responsibility to any person or entity with respect to any loss or damage caused directly or indirectly by the information in this publication.

Sections of Chapter 4 first appeared in the publication *EvoLLLution*.[1]
A version of Chapter 5 originally appeared in the publication *EvoLLLution*.[2]
Sections of Chapter 6 originally appeared in the publication *EvoLLLution*.[3]
Sections of Chapter 13 originally appeared in the publication *EvoLLLution*.[4]

ISBN-13: 978-1-957651-77-4

Library of Congress Control Number: 2024911273

Designed by Back Porch Creative LLC

INDIE BOOKS INTERNATIONAL®, INC.
2511 WOODLANDS WAY
OCEANSIDE, CA 92054
www.indiebooksintl.com

DEDICATION

To my wife, Candi Abeyta.
You've been the unwavering protagonist in every chapter of my life, guiding me with your strength and steadfast support.

CONTENTS

Foreword
By Executive Vice Chancellor Elizabeth Simmons   ix

Chapter 1	The Coming Renaissance Of Higher Education	1
Chapter 2	The Reinventing Lifelong Learning Model	11
Chapter 3	Career Changers	21
Chapter 4	Career Enhancers	25
Chapter 5	The Data On Lifelong Learning Beginning In Childhood	31
Chapter 6	Precollegiate Outreach	39
Chapter 7	High School Research Scholars	45
Chapter 8	High School Academic Connections Residence Programs	53
Chapter 9	STEAM Education Made Accessible: Ride, Sally, Ride!	57
Chapter 10	Futures	61
Chapter 11	Retirement Learning	67
Chapter 12	TV/Internet	71
Chapter 13	Professional Development For Teachers	75
Chapter 14	Guests For College Credit	79
Chapter 15	Parent University	87

Chapter 16	Mexico And Latin America	91
Chapter 17	Overcoming Stop-Outs	97
Chapter 18	Enhancing Campus Objectives	101

Appendices

Acknowledgments	103
About The Author	105
Works Cited And Author's Notes	107
Index	115

Foreword

By Executive Vice Chancellor Elizabeth Simmons, UC San Diego

Profound shifts in the landscape of public higher education are challenging us to rethink our approach to continuing education.

Our university, UC San Diego, once had a traditional view of University Extension as an outward-facing, auxiliary enterprise, fundamentally distinct from the university's academic core. Over a forty-year history of operating in this mode, our University Extension became successful and visible, boasting deep community networks and providing demonstrable impact.

However, UC San Diego has come to see that a connected, collaborative vision of extended studies' role within the university can render it an even more valuable and powerful partner in pursuing the institution's mission.

As universities strive to serve the nation's shifting needs, we must move beyond models solely based on traditional student populations and conventional pathways into higher education. Yet making the change is a daunting task.

The author, Edward Abeyta, PhD, an associate dean with our Division of Extended Studies, suggests this is a fixable problem. Ed likes to say we need to focus on "twinkle-to-wrinkle solutions," including everyone from preschoolers to senior citizens in the mix.

Over the past five years, Ed and his colleagues have worked with campus partners to first evolve and then enact a new vision for Extension, dovetailed with our view of the role of the modern public research university as being student-centered, research-focused, and service-oriented, with a strong emphasis on multidirectional community engagement.

Anyone aspiring to elevate their university's continuing education and community-serving roles will find something of direct interest and value in this volume. The approaches discussed here reflect pragmatic programs that have been field tested, evaluated, and refined on campus and throughout our region.

As always, Ed's infectious enthusiasm, his decades of experience, and his dedication to connecting members of historically marginalized communities to career-relevant educational opportunities come through clearly. We at UC San Diego count ourselves very lucky to have him on our leadership team.

Elizabeth H. Simmons
Executive Vice Chancellor
Distinguished Professor of Physics
University of California (UC) San Diego
March 2024

Chapter 1
The Coming Renaissance Of Higher Education

This is a renaissance moment for higher education. We educators are on the cusp of a season of opportunity that the world has not seen in a long time.

Historians, business leaders, and our own experience would suggest that we're entering into an era like the Renaissance.

The choice is a stark one of fantastic opportunity and significant risk. A coming disruption of higher education has already begun.

After every major world event—usually tragic—like the bubonic plague or World War II—there was a rebirth: a time of incredible innovation, creativity, and an economic boon.

Here is what happens during a renaissance. People are put into a circumstance both out of their control and far beyond what they could have possibly imagined. Everything changes rapidly and with little warning. Our existence has been threatened in each of the historic events that have led to a renaissance.

Disruption This Way Comes

To paraphrase the science fiction author Ray Bradbury, something disruptive this way comes. During the pandemic, we faced our own mortality. We lost loved ones. And we knew life would not be the same as it was during the former times.

Looking back in history to previous former times, though the bubonic plague was grim, there was an unseen benefit. The plague helped create the conditions necessary for the greatest post-pandemic recovery of all time—the global Renaissance.

Priorities changed, and new business models emerged. Necessity inspired a whole new level of innovation and creativity. Higher education certainly had an upheaval.

The Renaissance became known for its art, music, and architecture. The period is commonly associated with Michelangelo's painting of the ceiling of the Sistine Chapel and his majestic statue, *David*, Gutenberg's printing press, and Leonardo da Vinci's *Mona Lisa*.

The Renaissance laid the foundation for the very fabric of our modern society. As feudalism died along with the plague, individual contributors took its place. Merchants and commerce, banking, property investments, and advances in science propelled people forward.

A common misperception is that higher education was watching from the sidelines. Paul F. Grendler, an emeritus professor in the history department at the University of Toronto, corrects that assumption.

> *A persistent view holds that Renaissance universities were conservative homes of outmoded knowledge…Nothing could be further from the truth. Universities across Europe played extraordinarily significant roles in the Renaissance and the*

Reformation. They hosted innovative research in many fields and changed forever European religion and society.[5]

This was a moment in time when people had to reinvent, including higher education. They had to try new things. They had to do what had never been done before.

The crisis was the catalyst for dramatic change, creativity, and the birth of many new and lasting innovations.

History provides other examples.

Following World War II, we also experienced a renaissance. Wages were 50 percent higher than they had been five years prior, and unemployment was completely eliminated. Shipyards cut the time it took to build a ship from 365 days to less than a week. The flu vaccine was invented in the '40s, as was the first modern computer.

Roger L. Geiger, the Distinguished Professor Emeritus of Education at Pennsylvania State University, chronicles the rebirth of American education following World War II. His books include *The History of American Higher Education: Learning and Culture from the Founding to World War II* and *American Higher Education since World War II: A History.*[6]

Geiger notes that American higher education is nearly four centuries old. But in the decades after World War II, as government and social support surged and enrollments exploded, the role of colleges and universities in American society changed dramatically.

Geiger examines this remarkable transformation, taking readers from the G.I. Bill and the postwar expansion of higher education to the social upheaval of the 1960s and 1970s, including desegregation and coeducation.[7]

The question is: what part will we play? Are we the leaders who will get challenged and replaced, or are we the innovators who will create new business models and drive innovation and creativity?

Calling All Innovators

Continuing education has long embraced the concept of lifelong learning. The premise of lifelong learning is grounded in the idea that learning is an ongoing, voluntary, and self-motivated pursuit of knowledge for personal or professional reasons.

Many economists believe lifelong learning is critical to sustaining a competitive and skilled workforce. Although continuing education professionals have traditionally focused on the life stages of adults twenty-five and older, could continuing education be well-positioned to complement secondary education institutions in the twenty-first century?

What does obtaining a degree get you these days in the United States? Is it worth it? How soon does obsolescence kick in on what we learn in college?

Finding answers to these questions leads to a simple yet complicated conclusion. Lifelong learning has never been more important to build the life you want and keep skills and knowledge relevant within and beyond your chosen profession.

Over the past decade, a search for answers has brought me to a place of hope and anticipation. I see a renaissance on the horizon for higher education, one in which a four-year degree is a starting point, but just that. Finding our way along this path will require deep thinking and careful planning.

Reinventing lifelong learning is a major adaptive challenge for educators in the decentralized landscape of the US system of higher education.

> **Education Approaches A $3 Trillion Market**
>
> According to a 2023 research study from Facts & Factors, the US education market was estimated at $1.41 trillion in 2021 and was expected to reach $3.12 trillion by 2025. The US education market was expected to grow at a compound annual growth rate of 4.21 percent from 2022 to 2030.[8]
>
> Education is the method or mode of learning through particular habits, knowledge, values, skills, and beliefs. It is a key tool for growth and reducing poverty, enhancing health, maintaining peace, acquiring knowledge, and maintaining gender parity. Education in the US is decentralized and based on the federal constitution.

Relevancy: Innovate, Evolve, Or Perish

Charles Darwin reportedly once said, "It is not the biggest, the brightest, or the best that will survive but those who adapt the quickest."

For colleges and universities, this adaptation tends to occur slowly—some might say "intentionally"—and because of significant pushes from external forces. Fortunately, many institutions have divisions on their campuses that can help create internal pushes for change: their nontraditional divisions. Termed as Continuing Education, Extension, Professional Studies, and more, these divisions serve nontraditional audiences and tend to be on the leading edge of changes in the postsecondary space.

One major priority for nontraditional divisions is relevance in everything they do. From programming to credentials, every single piece of the educational product on offer must align with a stated and demanded need.

This focus on relevance is something most universities would significantly benefit from adopting overall, as clearly indicated by the value of traditional credentials alone. As millions of college students walk across graduation stages, the painful message for many graduates emerges—a college degree does not necessarily equate to workforce readiness. Postsecondary institutions are on notice that workforce relevancy is the key to these graduates' sustained workforce success.

Postsecondary education credentials continue to be under scrutiny by employers who find recent graduates do not have the workforce-readiness skills to make an impact. The disconnect between higher education and industry is not a new phenomenon. In 2013 a Gallup poll, sponsored by the Lumina Foundation, uncovered that only 14 percent of Americans and 11 percent of industry leaders strongly agreed that college graduates have the necessary skills and competencies to succeed in the workplace.[9] In contrast, another 2013 Gallup poll for Inside Higher Ed indicated that 96 percent of academic officers believed that they were very or somewhat effectively preparing students for the workforce.[10]

This incongruence has affected the industry to the point where companies must compete by recruiting skilled talent to fill job openings connected to new projects and initiatives. Today's employers are expecting practical skills, not just theory. Our new graduates must demonstrate their ability to learn and execute but they are not equipped, and they know it. Jaimie Francis and Zac Auter note that only "35 percent of college students say they are prepared for a job, and over half of recent graduates are unemployed or underemployed."[11]

Relevant education in context will not happen until business leaders, academic leaders, and policymakers work together to make it so. That's our challenge, and the Gallup/Lumina surveys are our wake-up call.

In a 2021 article in the *Harvard Business Review*, researcher John Hagel III examined the motivation of workers toward lifelong learning, "We discovered that rather than fear, employees who learned and grew in this way tended to exhibit what we have called the *passion of the explorer*. This passion is a very powerful motivator for learning."[12]

Where can this passion start? Throughout college, students ought to be able to clearly see their pathway toward gaining both skills and knowledge. And when students graduate, employers should be able to determine what sets of skills and knowledge they bring to the workplace. Achieving both of these will help address the looming confidence gap and build the pipeline of talent necessary for our students and nation to thrive.

At the University of California San Diego (UC San Diego), we're attempting to address the disconnect between academia and industry to promote student success and development by incorporating the following twelve competencies:

- critical thinking and problem-solving
- research ability
- oral, written, and digital communication
- teamwork and cross-cultural collaboration
- understanding global context
- leadership
- professionalism and integrity
- self-reflection

- career development
- digital information fluency
- civic engagement and social responsibility
- innovation and entrepreneurial thinking

These competencies and learning outcomes[13] were created to align with the:

- American Association of Colleges and Universities (AAC&U) VALUE Learning Outcomes
- Council for the Advancement of Standards (CAS) in Higher Education student learning and development outcomes
- WASC Senior College and University Commission core competencies
- National Association of Colleges and Employers (NACE) Career Readiness Competencies

Credit: Teaching + Learning Commons

The UC San Diego Education Initiative Working Group will review these competencies every four years to ensure they remain relevant to industry and key postsecondary agencies, associations, and accrediting agencies.

When students have graduated, employers should be able to determine what sets of skills and knowledge they bring to the workplace. Achieving both of these will help address the looming confidence gap and build the pipeline of talent necessary for our students and nation to thrive. And despite a century of experience with higher education, our system tells us far too little about what a college degree or other postsecondary credential means.

As a result, many postsecondary institutions are exploring a Co-Curricular Record (CCR). A CCR is a method of capturing student achievements in opportunities beyond the classroom, including a brief description of the skills developed on an official record. UC San Diego has developed the Co-Curricular Record to recognize student involvement in:

- research and academic life
- student and campus engagement
- community-based and global learning
- professional and career development

The purpose of the CCR is to demonstrate the value of engaging in opportunities beyond the classroom and to help students reflect on and articulate the competencies and skills they have developed. This approach seeks to provide industry additional insights into a graduate's skills, knowledge, and abilities not visible in a traditional transcript.

As our nation's labor market continues to transform, it's more critical than ever that everyone has access to an education that equips them to thrive in our twenty-first-century economy. Preparing our talent pipeline requires a collaborative effort among leaders in academia, industry, and government to figure out the best ways to identify, reward, and motivate top agile talent while supporting the constant need to learn. Each must both evolve to stay competitive.

The US Department of Labor's Brent Parton noted the necessity of "continual training throughout a person's lifetime—to keep current in a career, to learn how to complement rising levels of automation, and to gain skills for new work." He predicted, "workers will likely consume this lifelong learning in short spurts when they need it, rather than in lengthy blocks of time as they do now when it often takes months or years to complete certificates and degrees."[14]

The message is clear: individuals must constantly hone and enhance their skills to remain relevant in the workforce. As a society, we must figure out how to rapidly update workforce skills and competencies on an ongoing basis to remain globally competitive, avoid long periods of high unemployment, and continually evolve our workforce. Adapting to this mindset of continuous learning and relevance is perhaps America's biggest challenge in staying competitive.

Chapter 2

The Reinventing Lifelong Learning Model

How did UC San Diego find its way toward this new lifelong learning model? We looked at the data and responded. We responded to a perception gap regarding workplace preparedness.

I first started looking at this kind of data in the early 2000s and have seen too little change over the past decades.[15] That's why I find this reinvention process a matter of urgency.

Ashely Finley, vice president for research and senior adviser at the American Association of Colleges and Universities (AAC&U) and author of a 2021 AAC&U skills preparedness report,[16] says, "The bottom line is that at a time when colleges and universities might be tempted to retrench resources, specifically to limit breadth of learning and skill development, they should not."[17]

Here are some key findings from the report:

- "Employers have confidence in higher education and value the college degree.
- A liberal education provides the knowledge and skills employers view as important for career success.

- Personal aptitudes and mindsets also play an important role in career success.
- Completion of active and applied learning experiences gives job applicants a clear advantage.
- Both breadth and depth of learning are needed for long-term career success."[18]

The study's results are not surprising. Employers value translatable, adaptable skills. But are higher education institutions providing this? What are students looking for and receiving from their education as it currently exists?

The Changing Relationship With Students

Too often, students feel they need to go to the altar, kneel down, and beg, "God, please let me get into this institution—this cathedral of learning—because that's my ticket. It's the Wonka ticket. Only then will I go on to be successful in life." Corporations should also have just as much alarm because they're relying on institutions; higher learning institutions are the pipeline for the future.

Something is really going on here when we look in the mirror. If I'm higher education, I'm looking good, and I'm going to give myself an A+. But in that same mirror, someone beside me looks and says, "Oh no, you've got it all wrong. I'm giving you an F." If we're preparing our workforce for the twenty-first century, we've got a problem. We have not built a model of lifelong learning as a basic assumption of what higher education is meant to offer.

So, where do we go from here?

For too long, we've been second to traditional higher education. Not because we were put there but because sometimes we've placed ourselves there. Today, as continuing education folks, we have an opportunity to flip the equation. It starts with us having a voice in starting our own rankings. The model is traditional, it's outdated; it was built on an outdated time. It's not just about research and federal dollars. It's more than that. It's about work preparedness.

To move forward from this model, we need to know one thing. Higher education institutions may rank themselves well at job placement, but that doesn't mean students are prepared for the job.

We have the power to start looking at what the criteria of workforce preparedness is, working with our stakeholders in industry. The communities we serve should know the investment made in tax dollars is getting a high return on this investment.

The lifelong business of learning means we start before students get to college, and we may get them for the rest of their lifetime.

We are, in continuing education, bridge builders. We know how to connect to corporations.

Who are institutions turning to when all these things happen and we don't have any money? Continuing education. Why? Because they know how to run things on a leaner budget, they know how to get results, and they're business minded. They actually know how to connect to industry.

When you get to college, the fact of the matter is, the traditional model is not working. Student debt continues to grow, and efforts to curb or mitigate student debt are met with understandable political headwinds (why should this loan be forgiven when I still owe x for y?) We strapped so much debt onto students; they came out of college and wanted to live the American dream. The American dream has changed because it was built on an old model. This is an American problem because it's an economic and workforce problem.

STEAM Power

This leads to the concept of STEAM (science, technology, engineering, arts, and math) education and of left brain/right brain collaboration. The left brain is STEM, which is problem-solving convergent thinking. The right brain is where ideas come from, which is divergent thinking. The right brain is messy by design. It's crazy, it's where love happens, it's about thinking about possibilities.

In fact, the original STEM (which later became STEAM with the addition of the arts) principle was based on an engineer, Leonardo Da Vinci, who was not an engineer by training.[19] He was a naturalist; he went out and looked at nature and said, "How can I apply these principles in a way that transfers knowledge into the workplace?"

What comes with mixing arts with STEM is that solving problems means collaboration. Today, collaboration is a way in which we can look at better innovations in working politically from right to left and also a way we can bridge continuing education with higher education.

There are a lot of lessons we can learn from continuing education. We are bridge builders. We need to flip the equation. We need to think about moving from STEM to STEAM. We have the opportunity to go beyond thinking we're just second to anybody. We are the leaders; we get the students for the rest of their lifetimes and lend them to higher education institutions. Together, harmony occurs, and we're making a better workforce for tomorrow.

Experience Design: Seeing Students As Customers

The data and messages from industry are clear: there's more competition in continuing education and alternatives.

If you're going to have workforce development programming, something has to separate you from the competition. One area is service and customer service—that's the differentiator. It's all about the experience now. Tech companies like Google have been signaling for years that if higher ed wasn't going to do it, then they would. Now we're here.

The competition isn't just about institutions but industry moving into our markets and moving forward without us. That's why things are rapidly changing in customer service.

The landscape of learning and work has changed immensely over the last fifty years. Here's the challenge: you can talk about the student experience in terms of amenities, the vibe, and social networks, but since the cost of higher ed has increased so much, people are thinking of another route because they don't want to be in debt. They would sacrifice some of those amenities and social networks to get some of the commoditized areas of education out of the way. They can do this through community college, but at the end of the day, it's not the institution driving it—students are. Our traditional models have forced our institutions to start thinking differently because customers demand it.

Where does that leave educators? Every campus has something unique that makes it a viable product. There are a lot of options out there, so how do you differentiate? At the end of the day, it depends on the institution's president and system and their objectives. At the University of California, each campus is a land-grant institution. "Land-grant universities distinguish themselves from other institutions by directing their collective brainpower and resources toward research that addresses society's economic, political or social problems," according to Purdue University.[20] A land-grant institution is to share what it learns with the public in an effort to improve its citizens and communities. Our job is to connect to the community and enhance it.

So, a differentiation is: are the graduates we're producing contributing to society?

Lifelong Learning Starts Before College

We're entering new demographics in America. Jobs are rapidly changing—jobs that people of diverse cultures and nationalities do. When you start thinking about rapid changes and what we contribute, it's not just about offering a four-year degree. It's about how we connect with students before they get to an institution. That's lifelong learning.

The talent pipeline starts in early childhood; that's malleable learning. There are so many components to the various learning stages. When we talk about differentiating, it's not about a one-and-done experience. It's creating an affinity to the institution as their partner for life.

It's not their fault, but faculty have a different mindset based on their own experiences with more traditional processes. In many cases, they believe higher learning is a cathedral and want to protect it. There are ways to maintain faculty integrity and quality, but you can layer on things that complement that experience through services, support, and engagement.

It's really about progressing and adapting—as we learned from the pandemic. We had to covet a structure we were comfortable with. As an institution, we can't do away with the integrity of our academic systems, but we can adjust to the population we serve. We must reexamine our practices because we're either adapting or dying.

Education is one of the biggest investments parents or students will make, alongside something like a house. We've noticed that our students face a tedious, challenging process when applying. So, my suggestion is that they shouldn't be left alone to do this.

Institutions can start developing a talent pipeline connected to school districts and educators that allows people to take a couple of courses. We can use lifelong learning as extensions. Students would have a better idea of their investment before they enter college. They can get in and out. It's a more holistic approach and will require us to reexamine our strategy. It's not just about enrolling students to get bums in the seats. It's about building relationships that can foster an affinity that benefits the institution and enhances our greater community.

Examples Of Experience Design

In some cases, this notion of transactional vs. transformational—graduate institutions whose missions teams take to schools and present are transactional.

The transactional approach is more concerned with transactions, efficiency, and maintaining order. You can see this when educators present a topic in the community with little follow-up or impact. Conversely, a transformational approach is about inspiring change, fostering innovation, and achieving long-term goals.

Continuing education can provide transformational experiences via programs, courses, and events to engage students before they seek to apply for college or provide parents a deeper education in preparing them to support their child as they make decisions post high school graduation.

Transactional Business Model	Transformational Business Model
• Primarily concerned with efficient processes and cost-effectiveness.	• Focuses on long-term goals, innovation, and adaptability.
• Short-term oriented and focuses on immediate gains.	• Seeks to bring about significant product, service, or market changes.
• Often involves routine transactions and well-established procedures.	• Values creativity, disruption, and staying ahead of the competition.

There are some short, four-day experiences that move the needle toward transformational because as students experience something, they connect more to it.

I'm learning about institutions connecting with parents through a concept I've nicknamed Parent University. The notion is to offer classes to parents through continuing education that help prepare them to support their child through college and into the workforce. That's transformational because it brings in the whole family. They're engaged, and everyone evolves together.

Further, students don't need to wait to start continuing education. They can finish a certificate before graduating high school or going to college. It instills the seed of getting out of the K–12 school system and connecting to a university. Dual enrollment already exists, but mainly academics participate. Look at the skills and knowledge we teach adults. These transformational elements can foster a greater impact and connection to the university for both parents and communities.

I believe education is a human right, and the investment in connecting with individuals and the community creates the basis for a healthy workforce. It lifts up jobs and creates a greater understanding of each other. This investment can help bridge the divide in our country. We need the ability to attack ideas and not each other. We're at a moment when investment can be a catalyst for positive change in communities and industries.

Ten years ago, we said that if we didn't do it, industry would. We thought we were doing a great job, but speaking to industry, some of them thought we weren't doing so great. Industry leaders said they would have to fix what we didn't in terms of the skilled worker. So, we have a lot of work to do.

Knowledge on demand is powerful. If you're not planning for the future in customer service—which is a differentiator—then guess what? You may be overcome by the wave ahead of you. You need to respond, not react.

Chapter 3

Career Changers

The year was 2008; the place was San Diego, California. Leslie Widner was passionate about teaching and earned a college degree and a teaching credential.

Unfortunately for Widner and other hopeful educators during the Great Recession, teaching jobs were few and far between. Frustrated and desperate, Widner took a job as a front-office supervisor at a large hotel chain.

Once there, she ignited her second passion: caring for the environment.

"I saw such an enormous amount of waste there," said Widner about the hotel. "They had no recycling at all and probably used a ream of paper a day."

She set up a recycling program at the hotel and soon began researching continuing education curricula locally for a program that would expand her expertise.

While reading an article about green events in San Diego, Widner came across the Sustainable Business Practices certificate program at UC San Diego.

"Sustainability is all about the three Es," said Widner. "Environment, education, and equity."

Widner admits to being intimidated at first. But her professors were knowledgeable, kind, and encouraging. They persuaded her to share her experiences in class and to stick with it.

Fortuitously, an internship facilitated by the program helped Widner land a job as soon as she obtained her certificate. That internship and her newly obtained sustainable business practices certificate opened the door to a job at a company providing composting services and education to schools, special events, and businesses.

One of Widner's responsibilities was to go into school lunchrooms and show children how they can have minimal impact on the environment. Widner was able to combine both passions: teaching and acting as a steward for the environment.

Widner was happy to offer advice to others thinking about or, perhaps, being forced to make a career change.

"Look at your life and look at the consistencies in it," said Widner in 2009. "Find something you are already passionate about, research a program that will enhance your knowledge, go for it, and don't even worry about the economy."

Career Changers Need Continuing Education

Career changers are individuals who decide to transition from one career field to another. They may have different motivations for making this change, such as wanting to pursue a new passion or interest, seeking better job opportunities, or finding a career that aligns better with their values and goals.

Career changers may face unique challenges such as lack of experience in the new field, difficulty adjusting to a new work environment, and uncertainty about their career path. However, they may also bring valuable skills and experiences from their previous careers that can be applied to their new roles.

Career changers may need to undergo additional education or training to acquire the necessary skills and knowledge for their new career. They may also need to network with professionals in their new field and gain relevant work experience through internships or volunteering.

Chapter 4

Career Enhancers

One day, Ellen Ray decided she was getting older and wanted to enhance her skills on the job.

For twenty-five years, Ray had worked for the Orange County Sanitation District, where she began her career as a mechanic. Eventually she became a certified crane-and-equipment operator and then, at the request of her safety manager, earned a certificate to train other employees on operating small cranes.

She liked her training so much that she pursued her safety-training career through a specialized US Occupational Safety and Health Administration (OSHA) certificate program in occupational health and safety.

UC San Diego was one of four original OSHA Training Institute Education Centers established by the US Department of Labor. We offer high-quality, standards-based OSHA training in California, Arizona, Nevada, and Hawaii.

Since 1992, thousands of safety and health professionals like Ray have attended courses and earned our Professional Safety and Health Officer Certificate.[21]

"Until I went through the OSHA program, I didn't realize there was so much more for me to learn and know," confessed Ray.[22]

Ray was promoted to oversee construction projects for the Orange County Sanitation District.

"Things are changing all the time," said Ray. "Even with all the training on any given day, somebody will have fallen off a ladder or be injured in a trench. As far as I'm concerned, even one person getting injured is one too many. We really try to push safety. I want people, when they come to work, to know that they are trained, and feel comfortable enough to do their job."

She said she wanted workers to know that the employer has done everything it can to mitigate any hazards.

"At the end of the day, they can go home to their families in one piece," said Ray. "I do feel like I make a difference.

Adapting For The Future Of Work

The rate of change in the world of work and culture at large is not slowing down. In my view, a BS or BA degree is, by necessity, the first stage in adapting skills to meet new opportunities. Continuing-education opportunities are a way for colleges and universities to help people adapt and train for the future of work.

There are more students than ever attending some form of postsecondary education institution to earn a credential that enhances their opportunities to compete for jobs. In fact, the education level for individuals aged twenty-five to thirty-four from 1940 to 2021 increased from 6 percent to 36 percent. Now the federal government is leading the charge to drive that completion rate up to 60 percent across the United States.[23]

If this trend continues, one must question the value of a postsecondary degree if such a high percentage of people hold one. How can one build their competitive edge beyond that degree?

There is an overabundance of statistics to illustrate the private and societal returns on postsecondary education. A number of reports point out the positive returns on education, showcasing the correlation of education and financial and social returns to the individual and other returns to society at large.[24] Other benefits from postsecondary education include: increased tax revenues at all government levels, higher salaries and benefits, reduced crime rates, and improved quality of life. Additionally, the link between high-quality education and economic growth has been made by numerous researchers.[25]

The relationship between the American economy and its system of postsecondary education has been symbiotic over the years. During times of economic growth, enrollment in higher education tends to decline because the supply of jobs outweighs the demand for jobs, providing more opportunities for work and higher pay, thus decreasing the demand for education. When the economy is in recession, enrollment in higher education tends to increase because the labor market reduces hiring, thereby forcing individuals to attain more credentials to remain competitive in the workforce.

Not all researchers believe more education contributes to economic growth. For example, James Murphy asserts that the dogmatic belief that postsecondary growth has an impact on economic success is false. He points out three major problems with this belief:

- It overemphasizes the economy's need for college and university graduates.
- It hyperbolizes the significance of postsecondary graduates in economic booms.
- It exaggerates the capacity of college and university education to shape the labor market for the needs of employers and growing industries.[26]

Alison Wolf also questions the connection between degree attainment and economic growth. She notes, "we cannot use rates of return to prove that more educational spending must be a good idea. On the contrary: it is no more self-evident that, since some education makes some of us rich, more would make more of us richer than it is that 'two aspirin good' means 'five aspirin better.'"[27]

Getting a college degree and an elite job is very beneficial, but for everyone who does not get a four-year degree, the future is obscure. There is an increasing divide between highly educated and undereducated labor. The median annual salary for a mechanical engineer was in the mid-$90Ks in 2022.[28]

And while lower-skilled and blue-collar jobs are making headway, the earning potential is still significantly higher with a bachelor's degree than with a high school diploma. According to the Social Security Administration, men who hold bachelor's degrees receive median lifetime earnings of approximately $900,000 more than those who are only high school graduates. Female earners with bachelor's degrees receive $630,000 more.[29]

Historically, the labor market rewards postsecondary degrees, but there is little empirical evidence that postsecondary degrees are indicators of higher skill levels. Continuing-education providers have a great opportunity to weigh in on this debate, given the evidence that specific certificate and credential programs provide relevant industry skills, but there is insufficient evidence to say that the ever-evolving knowledge economy requires higher levels of education.

If students are pushed to simply earn degrees regardless of the content, the value of a postsecondary degree in the years ahead will probably decline. Decreasing enrollment numbers across higher education reflect this trend. However, if students are encouraged to pursue a degree that leads to a positive workforce outcome, the value is definitely there.

Beyond the degree, policymakers and leaders in continuing education have the opportunity to open the door to discussions about what skills are needed for the future and to discuss measuring relevancy of what postsecondary graduates are able to do when they are awarded a postsecondary degree in any field. Future conversation must focus on improving the link between education and the workforce.

Chapter 5

The Data On Lifelong Learning From Childhood Onward

It is important to have benchmark standards for the knowledge and skills students are expected to master in a given subject at a given grade level. Today, all states have developed and implemented standards; in many cases, however, these standards do not reflect the knowledge and skills needed for success after high school, either in further education or in a job. Nationally, as many as six of every ten new community college students now take remedial courses,[30] and industry frequently comments on the inadequate preparation of high school graduates. Our high school students are underprepared and paying the price when they arrive at college.

National data suggests more than half of college-bound students are undecided about their major or decide to switch majors. Writing in *Psychology Today* in 2021, University of South Carolina sociology professor and author Deborah Cohan says it is very common for college students not to know what they want to major in and to change their major multiple times.[31]

The real dilemma is these students are still expected to select schools and apply to and start degree programs without fully knowing where they want to end up. Continuing-education pre-college programs, like at Brown University, offer high school students the means to avoid this problem and many other barriers college students face once they arrive on a college campus.

Brown University once developed a diverse portfolio of pre-college programming for secondary students to enroll in online. These programs enable students to a) prepare for the academic challenges during the first year of college; b) confirm their interest in a profession or field of study; and c) gain exposure to college before graduating from high school. The courses continue to evolve but once included titles like Exploring Medicine: Do You Want To Be A Doctor? and Introduction To Genetics And Epigenetics: We Are Not Just Our DNA!

In addition to offering college-prep programs, Columbia University School of Professional Studies once went a step further by offering a unique opportunity for academically exceptional local high school students to take college courses with Columbia University students and earn full college credit. The High School Visiting Student Program was created for high school juniors and seniors who have demonstrated academic excellence in their studies and are highly motivated to advance their academic careers. This program also continues to evolve.

Francesca Slade said, "I had completed enough math at my school to enable me to take calculus at Columbia over the summer. I enjoyed the class so much that I continued taking math, physics, and theoretical computer science classes. I have almost completed the requirements for a math major at Columbia. I just found out that I've been accepted to Cambridge and Yale, and I'm looking forward to starting college!"

Although further research investigating the impact of college-prep programs similar to Brown and Columbia needs to be conducted, the impact these programs have on lowering high school dropout rates, increasing persistence rates in college, and college graduation completion appears significant. Early engagement with institutions of higher learning makes sense, given the significant investment students and their families will likely make with their decision to attend college. The goal should be to ensure each student maximizes their return on investment in terms of obtaining their degree, obtaining a good job upon graduation, and avoiding significant student loan debt by increasing their ability to repay loans.

The national continuing-education professional associations, the US higher education system, and workforce development leaders should take note of the opportunity to embrace a paradigm shift in education. The current education system is based on an obsolete era, mirrored on the industrial revolution. Today, our next generation needs to be enabled to have core foundations of science, technology, engineering, and math while also being driven by the creative and innovative constructs of the liberal arts. And above all, continuing education should serve as a bridge between secondary, postsecondary, and lifelong education continuing into adulthood.

Lifelong learning does not begin as an adult; it is not measured throughout one's life by standardized testing, nor does it reach some endpoint. Lifelong learning starts as early as life itself begins. Continuing education professionals should understand that they have a duty to promote, communicate, and deliver programming starting in early life stages. If this is not achieved, the phrase "lifelong learning" is misleading—according to the prevailing wisdom right now, it is only for adults twenty-five and older. This notion needs to change—it is over our entire lives, not just a portion of our lives, that we should always be learning.

Work-Based Learning And Continuing Education: Connecting The K–12 Classroom To Real Life[32]

The next generation must be ready to transition into the workplace, or their jobs will go to someone else—in many cases, someone well-trained and in a far-off country. It is no secret the competition for jobs has expanded globally. While each of these statements might seem disquieting in nature, each is true, and each reemphasizes the necessity and urgency of preparing our graduates for a successful transition into the global workforce. Our students' competitive edge may rest in secondary and postsecondary institutions offering work-based learning programming that connects their learning to real life.

So, what is work-based learning? It is an educational strategy that links school-based instruction with real-life experiences in the workplace. It is a planned program of job training and work experiences such as job shadowing, informational interviews, workplace tours, and workplace mentoring. Additionally, programs could include components providing students with work experience through apprenticeships, volunteer work, service learning (learning through working in the community), school-based enterprises, on-the-job training, and paid employment.

Brennan and Little note that work-based learning has increasingly become an area of interest for the continuing education sector.[33] It has evolved into a means to support the personal and professional development of students who are already participating in the labor market, and the focus of the learning and development tends to be on the student's workplace activities.

Connecting learning to the workplace is nothing new in continuing education. In fact, it is common practice for continuing-education institutions to develop training, courses, and certificate programs based on input from industry professionals and company advisory boards. This collaborative effort results in relevant training for industry employees and a means for individuals to break into new or emerging jobs. Given the bond between continuing education and industry, it makes sense for educators across the teaching space—both in K–12 schools and in undergraduate institutions—to collaborate with the seasoned professionals in continuing education to bridge learning in the classroom to the real world.

Early work-based learning experiences can help students build crucial job-keeping skills, or soft skills. Many employers report wanting employees who are eager to learn, show respect, and take their job commitment seriously. While jobs in today's economy require that employees be able to solve problems, use technology, and be proficient in reading, writing, math, and speaking skills, it is the soft skills that seem to make the difference in whether or not an employer hires and keeps someone on the job. Specifically, employers want employees with positive social skills, including a strong work ethic, tolerance, self-discipline, self-respect, a friendly demeanor, and reliability.[34] This is not a secret to other countries that face the same challenge of developing the next generation of talent.

Countries worldwide are taking advantage of work-based learning to effectively train their future employees. Many countries have developed systematic policies for integrating young people into the workforce. Germany uses an apprenticeship work-based learning system that begins early and combines classroom and on-the-job instruction. In Japan, many employers agree to hire students referred to them by specific schools. Various organizations, administrative agencies, and policies in the US encourage work-based learning; however, the number of students participating in work-based learning and the quality of these programs differs from state to state, even from school district to school district.

High-quality work-based learning requires students to have the opportunity to engage meaningfully with the experiences offered and to reflect thoughtfully on their learning. It requires educators to link experiences to the classroom and to work closely with employers and communities to ensure students comprehend the standards to which they will be held as adults in the working world. Organizational structures and resources, instructor preparation, and employer engagement strategies must be aligned to facilitate this form of high-quality learning.

So, what are the benefits of work-based learning to students and educators? According to Rob Atterbury with ConnectED: the California Center for College and Career, students who participate in work-based learning connected to their school programs:

- show improved academic achievement
- realize the relevance of their education and apply acquired knowledge in a meaningful way
- have the opportunity to explore career options before selecting a college major
- increase self-confidence
- acquire real workplace experience and employability skills

- connect with an adult role model and mentor who provides employment support and could potentially lead to employment in the future
- are more likely to go on to some type of educational training after high school

As states explore ways to improve postsecondary student outcomes, work-based learning may factor significantly among the solutions. For this reason, it merits ongoing investigation and investment.[35]

Chapter 6

Precollegiate Outreach

University precollegiate programs serve as vital pipelines to higher education. High school recruitment has always played a major role in filling the ranks of undergraduate degree programs, yet these processes are often piecemeal at best, and institutions often don't have avenues for sharing best practices.

College prep programs are designed to provide students with sufficient skills, knowledge, and confidence to prepare for college while they're in middle or high school. One would imagine data on programs and students attending university precollegiate programs would be collected nationally and connected to the institutions' recruitment administration, but regrettably, they aren't. As a result, there's a shocking data leak in the precollegiate-to-college pipeline that needs to be addressed.

Given the national interest in remaining competitive in the global economy, promoting college access for all academically qualified students in the US remains a high priority today for both the public and private sectors. State governors, legislative committee members, and postsecondary education governing boards have joined together to discuss strategies for increasing college access and completion rates to respond to global market demands.[36]

In fact, nearly 70 percent of Fortune 100 companies allocate a proportion of their total philanthropic contributions to programs that support postsecondary enrollment.[37] One would think there would be a wealth of outcome data on these programs, but the information is limited.

At a macro level, there is neither a mandated reporting mechanism nor an accompanying central repository for information about pre-collegiate outreach programs operating in the US. At a micro level, research universities such as UC San Diego don't have a formalized transfer of pre-collegiate student data to admissions, nor is there an evaluation process to capture program impact and other data for administrators to review.

Over the past few decades, efforts have been made to understand the variety and scope of these programs at the national level. In 1992, the Department of Education commissioned Westat to identify examples of college-school partnerships meant to improve the academic preparation of middle and high school students. The resulting two-volume report was not meant to be a comprehensive directory, but it did provide details about forty-eight exemplary programs from twenty states and the District of Columbia, six of which were profiled via in-depth case studies.[38] Subsequent research in 2011 stated that national statistics continue to show substantial disparities in the postsecondary enrollment and completion rates between more and less advantaged groups.[39]

Additionally, the College Board inventory of pre-collegiate outreach programs from 1999 was initially published as a handbook and was ultimately used to develop a product, which evolved over time into an electronic database known today as the National College Access Program Directory. The directory stores information provided on a volunteer basis by pre-collegiate outreach program staff.

The 1999 College Board study revealed that pre-collegiate outreach programs vary by multiple characteristics, including the age or grade of their target student population, characteristics of students targeted, total number of students served, program goals, program services, primary location for delivery of services, parental involvement, services offered to parents, and evaluation activities.

Federally funded programs are an important national pre-collegiate outreach program landscape segment. First, the federal government has been the key player in developing pre-collegiate outreach programs.[40]

Federal expenditures for pre-collegiate outreach programs have been substantial and sustained over time. This level of funding has allowed large numbers of students to be served by federal pre-collegiate outreach programs.

Given the federal government's attention and investment in pre-collegiate programs, it seems odd that there isn't a clearinghouse to see taxpayers' return on investment in these programs. In future longitudinal studies sponsored by the National Center for Education Statistics, it will be useful to have more explicit questions such as exactly in which pre-collegiate outreach program students participated, whether they participated in multiple programs, and the number of hours per week that program participation entailed, and to use a verification system with the programs to confirm that administrators and students correctly identified pre-collegiate outreach programs.

The evidence highlights there is indeed a data leak in the precollegiate-to-college pipeline. The lack of a comprehensive, centralized, and annually updated repository for information on pre-collegiate outreach programs is an obstacle to rigorous research on this important topic. Taxpayers and education leaders must find a way to fix this problem, and awareness of the issues may be the first step.

Breaking Barriers To Higher Ed

In January 2014, the White House published a report, "Promising Models And A Call To Action," in which leading experts convened to identify the barriers to increasing college opportunities.[41]

Test preparation was one of the barriers noted in the report. Continuing education leaders can respond to this issue and position their units as a central resource to improving higher education access for low-income high school students.

More recently, the National College Attainment Network has been doing good work in closing equity gaps in postsecondary educational opportunities. They offer training and policy resources to do the much-needed work of sharing best practices and helping young people attend college regardless of economic and other circumstances.

Providing services like test preparation allows universities a strategic outreach opportunity while also ensuring all high-caliber students, regardless of their background, have the opportunity to receive quality test preparation often times otherwise available only to those who can afford it. Today, for-profit companies charge $200 to $3,000 for test prep instruction.⁴² The price is not something many low-middle-class families can afford.

Research by economists at the College Board has shown that the trade-off between cost and school quality is often favorable for low-income students, where small increases in cost come with large predicted increases in the likelihood of completion: "Compared to their high-income peers, students from low-income families are sometimes predicted to face a more appealing net price/completion trade-off associated with moving to a college with a higher average SAT score."⁴³

Regardless of income, college-prep programming matters. Research shows that activities such as SAT and ACT preparation, college awareness activities, and academic support services are integrated into the core curricula of well-funded schools and can be entirely missing or only sporadically available for high schools with less financial resources.⁴⁴

Continuing education divisions are positioned well to respond to the national call to address college preparation issues—including test prep. If students plan to spend four to six years in college, then continuing-education divisions have a role not only to prepare them for college but also to ensure these students continue their lifelong learning needs later in life.

Part of reinventing lifelong learning is about creating new pathways of access to educational resources, providing a pathway to college, and the tools for staying curious well beyond the college experience.

Chapter 7

High School Research Scholars

Let's bring the discussion of continuing education as a "test kitchen" into the discussion about high school outreach. At UC San Diego, we started the Research Scholars Program as a way to engage high school students with unparalleled educational opportunities that connect them directly with the intellectual capital of an internationally ranked research university, teaching highly sought-after skills that can make students more competitive candidates for college admissions, and providing individualized internship opportunities. Through the program, students take on the roles of researchers in projects that have real-world applications. This gives them the opportunity to experience research at the college level and begins to impart the importance of lifelong learning before they are even enrolled in a degree program.

Marine Science Researcher
A version of this story first appeared on the UC San Diego Extended Studies Blog.[45]

Students will connect with work that excites them, but an enthusiastic instructor makes all the difference in the world. Nicole Yen grew up in the San Francisco Bay Area, moved to coastal San Diego for college, and studied marine biology abroad in Australia. She has always been interested in animal research but felt a particular calling from the depths of the ocean.

Yen tries to impart that same sense of wonder and ocean stewardship to her students. Whether it's explaining the importance of salt marshes to prevent coastal flooding or of coral reefs as biologically diverse ecosystems, Yen guides students to understand how stressors like pollution can affect a multitude of environments.

"I don't think people realize how connected the ocean is to everything," she says. "It's a complicated web."

Now, Yen teaches a series of marine science classes for the UC San Diego Division of Extended Studies Research Scholars program. She says the classes are a natural evolution of her five years as a pre-college programs instructor.

"This is something I'm really excited about," says Yen. "The classes are foundational to give students a strong background knowledge and show them where they can apply that knowledge."

It helps that Yen is so earnest about ocean-focused academics. "Literally no one is more passionate about marine science than Nicole Yen," says Maysoon Dong, an associate director for the UC San Diego Division of Extended Studies Education and Community Outreach department.

The Research Scholars program gives high school students unique access to UC San Diego's research resources in bioengineering, life sciences, medicine, design thinking, and marine science.

Research Scholars is ushering in the next generation of environmental advocates by expanding the university's marine science studies to ninth through twelfth-grade students.

The coursework is crafted to be immersive with real-world applications. Yen encourages students to work together and individually to enhance their problem-solving, creative thinking, communication, and collaboration skills. Students can then use those skills to make informed decisions about their future vocations, earn pre-college credits, and be more competitive in college and internship applications.

What do high school students need to know to participate in this program? It doesn't matter if they have never taken a marine biology class or are already doing high-caliber research. The Research Scholars classes start with a broad overview of ocean sciences, then progress as far as publishing research in a scientific journal.

"For students who are interested in this field, it's so rare to get this kind of hands-on research experience," she says. "Getting the real experience is so valuable to see if it's something they could see themselves doing in college or as a career."

Yen says she works to make sure high school students participate directly in scientific research and writing rather than just doing back-end work for other researchers. She also wants to introduce students to working scientists of all backgrounds and orientations to visualize themselves in those roles.

"Scientists can be anyone. I want them to see, 'I can be a scientist, too,'" she says.

Academic Research Published[46]

This article, written by my colleague, Margaret King, tells one of my favorite stories from the Research Scholars program.

How does it feel to earn coauthor credit on a scientific journal article while you're still in high school? Pretty great, according to two students who accomplished that feat based on work they did after completing Research

Scholars courses from UC San Diego Division of Extended Studies and the Boz Life Science Research and Teaching Institute.

High school students Katherine "Katie" O'Connell and Natalie Olander were named on a journal article analyzing how various factors affect the likelihood that children will be diagnosed with ADHD (attention deficit/hyperactivity disorder). A third former Research Scholars student who is now in college, Sora Haagensen, also earned coauthor credit on the article.

Katie O'Connell was a senior at Poway High School in San Diego County at the time. "I never thought this would be something I would do in high school. I was also proud our work was successful because I worked very hard, and so did the rest of our team."

Natalie, who came to the program as a senior at Veritas High School in Newberg, Oregon, also expressed pride in the achievement. "Getting an article published is a big milestone for all scientists," she said. "To have already gotten listed as a co-author on a paper, it's phenomenal!"

For Sora, a graduate of The Bishop's School in La Jolla who now attends Brandeis University in Massachusetts, the ADHD article marks her second coauthor credit. Earlier, she contributed to an article about the genetics of a rare agave plant.

The three all took Research Scholars molecular biology classes from the Boz Institute in San Diego, which partners with the UC San Diego Division of Extended Studies to offer research immersion programs for high schoolers. Natalie took the course remotely through a sponsorship from the Oregon Bioscience Association.

The students enjoyed the coursework so much that they wanted to continue collaborating with Boz Institute scientists. In 2020, the three joined Boz researchers in an analysis of national data about ADHD. Diagnoses of the condition are surging, causing "a growing health crisis in the United States," the article states.

Through months of hard work, the researchers identified strong correlations among certain geographic and socioeconomic factors and cases of ADHD. The data clearly showed that ADHD diagnoses are more common among children living in the South and among those facing economic hardship and inhabiting unsafe neighborhoods.

The article appears in Scientific Reports, an online peer-reviewed journal published by Nature Portfolio. Former Boz researcher Kesten Bozinovic is lead author, and Boz scientist Zuying Feng, McLamb, and the three students are listed as coauthors, along with Boz Institute founder Goran Bozinovic.

The three students joined in weekly team meetings over Zoom and took on a significant role in the project. They surveyed previous scientific papers on the topic, then helped organize and analyze the data. They even contributed to writing the finished article.

For Olander, a biology class in her sophomore year sparked her interest in life sciences. "That's why I was really interested in the research immersion program because I loved biology so much," she explained. She aspires to become either a biomedical researcher or a physician-scientist.

As the researchers analyzed data, Natalie was excited to see patterns emerging. "I thought it was so neat that you could use a national data set and then find trends from it," she said. "It was really eye-opening, and it was a great experience. It gives me more knowledge stepping into other research and statistics."

Natalie took on the project in addition to her schoolwork and extracurricular activities—she runs cross-country and plays the piano. "Doing this required a time commitment, and I did it alongside homework," she said. "Our meetings would be after school, and I would fit in the work during the week."

She was gratified to be part of a team that divvied up tasks to reach a goal. "It was cool to see the collaboration and be in a professional environment," she said. "That has been a really helpful experience that has prepared me to continue in my research."

Katie said an interest in life science came naturally to her. An honors biology class in her freshman year deepened her interest, and the Research Scholars course convinced her to seek a career in the field. She plans to pursue a premed biology major with the goal of becoming a doctor.

The part of the project that was the most fun for her was helping to convert the study data into a series of elaborate charts and graphs. "That was quite difficult because we had so much data, and we had to figure out the best way to present it visually," she said. "I liked that a lot."

Like Natalie, Katie balanced the research with a busy schedule. At Poway High, she is vice president of the National Honor Society and president of the Academic Team. She has also received a Gold Award in Girl Scouts and plays violin for the San Diego Youth Symphony. "Since I really like doing the work, it didn't feel tedious or like a chore," she said. "That made it easier to commit."

She believes the experience will help her going forward. "When I tell people I have a published paper, they're super impressed," she said, "and I think it's cool that I'm able to cite myself now!"

Sora said the lessons she learned while working on the two journal articles are paying dividends for her in college. "The most important thing I learned from these experiences in publishing is not to give up when I think I have reached a dead end," she said. "There were many times when I sat scratching my head and feeling stuck, but neither I nor my coauthors ever threw in the towel."

The techniques she learned for organizing and interpreting difficult information are also proving to be a boon. "They have been a lifesaver for me in college while learning different languages," she said, noting that she had just finished her first semester of Japanese.

We are learning so much about early engagement through the high school Research Scholars program. It is just one way I see continuing education contributing in concrete ways to the progress of the students we serve and to academia itself.

Turning The Dream Into A Reality

The dream of college can seem daunting—especially for those who are the first in their family to consider the path of higher education.

A few years ago, UC San Diego Extension partnered with an organization called Barrio Logan College Institute (BLCI), an organization that provides college tutoring and mentoring for kids in elementary school and middle school.[47]

José Cruz, who served as executive director at the time, talks about teaching "active dreaming."

To enable this active dreaming, BLCI works with the entire family to prepare the students for college through a variety of after-school and summer programs.

Here are the basics of how they organize their programs. In the early years, instructors focus on reading and writing skills. As the students move into middle school, more behavioral education is incorporated to equip students with the tools to resist negative influences that can distract them from their educational goals. In high school, the focus shifts to "college knowledge" to ensure students choose the best courses and extracurricular activities to achieve their educational goals and bolster their college applications.

UC San Diego Division of Extended Studies works with BLCI by offering services like SAT instruction and summer programs designed to help prepare students both academically and socially for college. A partnership between a local university and a service organization like BLCI can have a big impact on lifelong learning. It starts kids on a leadership path, teaching them how to create solutions to problems large and small. It inspires kids from under-resourced neighborhoods to imagine the possibility of entering college and thriving beyond the completion of that degree.

Chapter 8

High School Academic Connections Residence Programs

Some students may be eager to be scholars and may have parents and others in their lives who expect higher education for their future and prepare them. But that is not the case for every middle and high school student. Many would benefit from preparation for the rigors of academic life as they consider college one of many options.

Some of San Diego's Barrio Logan College Institute students, for instance, participate in the Academic Connections program. Every summer UC San Diego Division of Extended Studies runs Academic Connections, a three-week summer program on the UC San Diego Campus as well as a number of week-long courses before the pandemic in Hawaii, New Mexico, and Arizona. To open up these transformative experiences to a wide variety of students, the UC San Diego Division of Extended Studies offers five scholarship spots for those who attend the Barrio Logan College Institute.

Guillermo Garcia received one of the scholarships to study at the past program in Los Alamos, New Mexico. There, he studied the region's geographic features and how rising temperatures affected its trees. He also took soil samples in desert and mountainous terrains.

"It was one of the best weeks I've ever had," Garcia said. "It also affected my studies. I wanted to do something with nature and engineering for a long time, and the program really helped me understand what I could do with that passion. When it comes to the future, my imagination is on full blast!"

Making The Path Clear

The majority of high school students are unprepared for the multiple demands of college work and the level of responsibility required by studying away from home. But there are new ways to taste the college experience and visit some of the most intriguing science venues in the West.

Academic Connections In The Biosphere[48]

Here are more details on two programs offered before the pandemic that the UC San Diego Division of Extended Studies hopes to reactivate.

Biosphere 2 is located north of Tucson, Arizona, at the base of the stunning Santa Catalina Mountains. This one-of-a-kind facility sits on a ridge at a cool elevation of nearly 4,000 feet and is surrounded by a magnificent natural desert preserve. The program with Biosphere 2, which Time Life Books recently named one of the fifty must-see "Wonders of the World," was offered prior to the pandemic in partnership with the University of Arizona. Academic Connections students will enjoy a unique adventure not found anywhere else. This is a rare opportunity to participate in real-time research on the future of our planet as it unfolds in the specially designed mini world.

The one-week program at the Los Alamos National Laboratory, a premier national security research institution, is offered in partnership with the University of New Mexico. The people of Los Alamos continually work on advanced technologies to provide the United States with the best scientific and engineering solutions to many of the nation's most crucial challenges. The primary responsibility of the Laboratory is to ensure the safety and reliability of the nation's defense program. Though the world is rapidly changing, this essential responsibility remains the core mission.

Those who choose the residential program at UC San Diego, long regarded as one of the nation's premier research universities, discover why the campus was named the "hottest" institution in the country for students to study science by *Newsweek* magazine.[49]

According to *Newsweek*, on a campus where a quarter of the more than $2 billion in revenue came from federal research funds, and where as of this writing five Nobel laureates are on the faculty, the science is quite serious. Former Chancellor Marye Anne Fox, an organic chemist, said welcoming undergrads into labs was a priority. "We want high school students to see what happens within the inner sanctum of science."

Academic Connections promises a taste of college and delivers with no time to waste. A typical day starts with breakfast at 7:00 a.m., lectures, workshops, and labs from 9:00 a.m. until 3:30 p.m. (including lunch), an afternoon activity, dinner, and then social activities from 7:30 p.m. until lights out at 11:00 p.m.

The message is clear. College will not be like the classes you experienced in high school. College is a full-time job, a community of learning, and a wonderful mix of social and intellectual experiences.

Academic Connections instructors, typically UC San Diego or other partner university doctoral students, tell it like it is.

Via a combination of lectures, labs, study halls, discussion roundtables, and guest speakers, the students get a peek into what college will be like. Courses are selected to represent some of the cutting-edge research fields UC San Diego offers in physical and social sciences, engineering, and arts and humanities.

Thanks to community partners, about 10 percent of students receive scholarships, which allows an opportunity for talented students who can benefit from the program but cannot afford to participate without financial assistance.

Chapter 9

STEAM Education Made Accessible: Ride, Sally, Ride!

Preparing students for college can take many forms. There is another example of this that I am proud of, especially as it relates to encouraging kids to consider STEAM-related education.

The Sally Ride Science Academy at UC San Diego educates hundreds of high school students in science, technology, engineering, art, and math in a program set up to deliver hands-on workshops on such topics as the science of earthquakes, space exploration, oceanography, robotics, 3D modeling, virtual reality, and more.

The Sally Ride Science Academy launched in 2016 as part of a partnership between UC San Diego and Sally Ride Science, an education company that Ride, the first American woman in space, her life partner Tam O'Shaughnessy, and Karen Flammer cofounded with two friends in 2001. Ride and the other founders were committed to expanding educational opportunities in the sciences, especially for girls and young women. Since 2016, the program has been developed to provide elementary, middle school, high school, and adult professional development programs.

Multiple organizations have been involved in making this project possible. UC San Diego Division of Extended Studies, the San Diego Super Computer Center, and Scripps Institution of Oceanography developed the curriculum for the Academy.

To ensure that a wide range of students could take part in the Sally Ride Science Academy, San Diego Unified School District worked with UC San Diego Division of Extended Studies to offer more than 150 scholarships to its students in sixth through twelfth grades, with a special focus on girls and young women.

At the opening of that first high school program, Cindy Marten, then superintendent of San Diego Unified School District, said Sally Ride Science at UC San Diego is helping to begin to close the gender gap in science and technology careers—something that is vitally important to ensure economic opportunity and regional prosperity.

"Half of the jobs today in our society require some type of technical background," Marten said. "In the next decade, it is predicted that the number could climb to 75 percent. We're not going to be able to fill those jobs unless we start attracting more and different students to those fields.

The Academy summer workshops include a variety of STEAM courses and allow students to immerse themselves in hands-on projects, assuming the roles of a geophysicist, ocean engineer, computer scientist, and beyond. The workshops also incorporate real-life stories from instructors conducting research in various areas to help inspire students to pursue careers in STEAM fields. The hands-on nature of the workshops is designed to engage students in these fields and encourage creativity and curiosity.

"This program is about more than technical know-how. It is about sparking an interest and then showing these students the path forward," Flammer said. "In this economy, technical know-how is not enough. You need creativity to innovate and that's why it is so important that we incorporate arts with science technology, engineering, and math."

Openness to experimentation and collaboration with local, national, and international organizations is the kind of creativity that is needed to keep reinventing lifelong learning.

Chapter 10

Futures

Continuing education at most colleges and universities typically consists of certificate programs offered to adults ages twenty-five to fifty-five. But what about exploring your options before committing to a postsecondary education? Choosing the right college or career pathway is not an easy decision.

The Power Of CTE

Career technical education (CTE) creates better outcomes for high school students who choose it. The California Department of Education (CDE) says CTE boosts graduation rates. While graduation rates overall in the state hover around 75 percent, graduation rates among CTE participants is 90 percent.[50]

Here are a few other interesting statistics from that same CDE fact sheet:

- Over 75 percent of students taking a CTE concentration in high school go on to enroll in postsecondary education and training after graduating.

- Eighty percent of students enrolled in both college prep and CTE programs met college and career readiness goals as opposed to just 63 percent of students in just college prep courses.
- Attendance in a CTE program more than doubles the rate of college entrance for minority students.
- Students who complete a blended academic–career curriculum are more likely to pursue postsecondary education, have a higher GPA in college, and are less likely to drop out of college in the first year.

The Futures Difference

The UC San Diego Division of Extended Studies Futures programs enable students to explore new interests and gain hands-on experience before they enter the workforce or apply for college. Each program is designed specifically for high school students. The coursework is taught by leading industry experts in high-demand fields. All programs culminate in an Award of Completion issued by UC San Diego Division of Extended Studies, which students may cite on college applications and résumés.

CTE is provided through many public schools for students in grades nine through twelve. A commitment to continuous improvement and innovation sets the Futures program apart.

Offering this kind of certificate program to high school students can be important for several reasons:

Skill development. Certificate programs can help students develop valuable skills that can be applied in the workplace or further education. These programs can provide hands-on experience and training in specific areas, such as technology, healthcare, or trades.

Career exploration. Certificate programs can help students explore potential career paths before committing to a specific field. This can help them make informed decisions about their future and increase their chances of success in their chosen career.

College readiness. Certificate programs can also prepare students for college-level coursework by providing them with foundational knowledge and skills. This can increase their readiness for higher education and improve their chances of academic success.

Job opportunities. Certificate programs can provide students with the skills and credentials needed to enter the workforce immediately after graduation. This can increase their chances of finding employment and starting their careers earlier.

At UC San Diego, we have tested many ways of setting up kids for lifelong learning success. The point is to think of extension programs as "test kitchens."

How Continuing Ed Can Be A Higher Ed Test Kitchen

As we developed the Futures program, we asked a fundamental question: can educators look to continuing education as a laboratory of change and evolution?

Higher education is resistant to change. The wide availability of—and then, in pandemic days, the necessity of—online education brought about unforeseen shifts that few were prepared for, and it is past time for the industry to be more open to future changes. Continuing education can play a key role in making this shift in thinking about program delivery.

While some might greet this reality with a sense of gloom and doom, I see so much room for optimism. With so great a need for lifelong learning opportunities, the current state of higher ed is one of the most exciting in recent times. Continuing education at a university has often been seen as an afterthought, ancillary to the institution's main purpose. Now, it is not a stretch to see it as a cornerstone of the ongoing relevance of higher education institutions.

One of the big events that has changed the course of education in recent years was the global pandemic. COVID-19 brought a seismic shift to so many industries, and higher ed is no exception. For an industry that is so set in its ways, a sudden monumental change to operations can be tough to manage.

Higher education needs to be more open to new ideas and innovations to continue to attract new learners. We are creatures of habit, but it is clear that institutions of higher learning cannot afford to do things the way we've always done them.

The mindset of protecting the "cathedral" was set in motion back when the Industrial Revolution kicked off, and some have hesitated to change their way of thinking.

Part of this process of reinvention needs to include new ideas for continuous learning for educators. Many have been in their roles for numerous years. Being seasoned in a profession is a good thing, but if we are expecting to educate for innovation, we need to start with ourselves. Continuing education can be a resource.

Continuing education is the test kitchen for new ideas that don't compromise the institution's integrity. Instead, continuing education adds complementary pieces to the higher education puzzle that may not have fit before. Changing the delivery method to the more digestible continuing education methods—shorter programs, smaller classes—can make foreign ideas fit easier at an institution.

We must be creative in delivering online, hybrid, or corporate education. That flexible delivery process and how we bring education to the community adds an amazing mindset that changes how we think about continuing education and how it connects to the area we serve.

Virtual or distant, boot camp or long form, hybrid or fully synchronous, there are options for educators to build a curriculum that will best serve the institution and, more importantly, the student.

The future is bright as we continue to connect people's needs and the resources available via lifelong learning. But this process can't just begin after someone graduates from college. There are opportunities long before that. High school is one of those places of opportunity we've been exploring here in San Diego.

Chapter 11

Retirement Learning

Finding pathways to college for young people is part of the equation, and providing opportunities for workforce-age people is vital, but lifelong learning doesn't stop when you leave the workforce. If anything, older adults have time, energy, and interest that should be explored. Road Scholar is a well-known example of how retirement learning can take people away from the familiar and explore and learn. But there are also many ways for local learning centers to build bridges with older adults.

UC San Diego has the Osher Lifelong Learning Institute (OLLI). The institute supports learning in retirement by offering a variety of educational programs and opportunities for older adults. OLLI provides a community for lifelong learning, with courses, workshops, and lectures on a wide range of topics, from history and literature to art and science.

Here's just one example of the power of lifelong learning in retirement.[51]

After seventy-nine-year-old Carol Roberts and her husband moved from Michigan to San Diego, she quickly realized she needed something to do. "As much as we like to see our friends and family, there are still plenty of hours in the day," she said. Then a newspaper blurb tipped her off to the Osher Lifelong Learning Institute.

Roberts attended lectures geared toward her interests, such as art history, and branched out to subjects she wasn't as familiar with, like astronomy. "This gives me a way to learn a little bit about a lot of things," she said. Roberts also worked her way up the Osher ladder. She served on the executive committee and was vice president of planning, which let her put the talents she garnered as an operator of a high-end tour business to further use. She organized highly anticipated field trips that coincided with the curriculum. Think of visiting a Jasper Johns exhibit after an art history lecture and walking tours accompanying in-depth lectures about local neighborhoods. Roberts eventually became president.

Roberts also enjoyed Osher's social aspect. Meeting people from all over with different talents and interests is part of the experience. Osher members learn for the sake of learning and take on some challenging subject matter. Past lectures include "International Legitimacy Lost? Global Order in the Age of 'America First,'" "Gender Sidelining and the Problem of Unactionable Discrimination," and "When Tiki Invaded San Diego." Lectures are also available in video form.

For Roberts, her love of learning came full circle. Her children asked her the same question she used to ask them: "Are you going to be late to school?"

Learning in retirement is important for several reasons:

Personal fulfillment. Many retirees want to continue learning and growing intellectually, and pursuing new interests and knowledge can bring a sense of personal fulfillment and satisfaction.

Cognitive health. Continuing to learn and engage in intellectual activities can help maintain cognitive health and prevent age-related decline in memory and other cognitive functions.

Social engagement. Learning in retirement can provide opportunities for social engagement and community involvement, which can help retirees stay connected and involved in their communities.

Career transition. Learning new skills and knowledge can also help retirees transition to new careers or pursue entrepreneurial endeavors.

Chapter 12

TV/Internet

One of the unique resources at UC San Diego is our UCTV platform administered by UC San Diego Division of Extended Studies. University of California Television (UCTV) is a public-serving media outlet featuring programming from throughout the University of California, the nation's premier research university, comprised of ten campuses, six health systems, three national labs, and affiliated institutions.

Launched in January 2000, this academic initiative embraces the core missions of the University of California—teaching, research, and public service—through quality, in-depth programming that brings to life the tremendous range of knowledge, culture, and dialogue generated on UC's diverse campuses.

Reaching the public through cable, online, YouTube, Apple Podcasts, Roku, and mobile apps, UCTV transports knowledge far beyond the campus borders and into the homes and lives of inquisitive viewers around the globe. UCTV has over one million YouTube subscribers, we're available via cable in four million homes, and we average five million monthly video hits/views, allowing programs created by UCTV's award-winning producers to contribute to thought around the world.

UCTV explores a broad spectrum of subjects, including science, health and medicine, public affairs, humanities, arts and music, business, education, and agriculture. Program formats include documentaries, faculty lectures, research symposia, artistic performances, and more.

During the pandemic, our department created the Education Channel to provide online resources for parents, educators, counselors, the college bound, policymakers, and those fifty and older. Supported by the California Department of Education and Community Outreach at the UC San Diego Division of Extended Studies, the Education Channel is a partner to educators, a resource for parents, and a way for students across the lifespan to continue learning and growing. Our evolving lineup of programs is designed to support educational goals and encourage creativity during the pandemic and beyond.

UCTV is a twenty-four-hour television channel presenting educational and enrichment programming from the campuses, national laboratories, and affiliated institutions of the University of California system. UCTV delivers noncommercial programming to a general audience, as well as specialized programming for health care professionals and teachers.

UCTV is based on the UC San Diego campus, where UCSD-TV is also located. UCTV collects programming from each of the ten University of California campuses (UC Berkeley, UC Davis, UC Irvine, UC Los Angeles, UC Merced, UC Riverside, UC San Diego, UC San Francisco, UC Santa Barbara, and UC Santa Cruz) and affiliated institutions (Lawrence Berkeley National Laboratory, Lawrence Livermore National Laboratory, Los Alamos National

Laboratory, UC Agriculture and Natural Resources, UC Office of the President, UC Center Sacramento, and UC Washington Center).

In 2023, UCTV launched the Visual and Productions Services initiative to support the evolving needs of our central campus, the Division of Extended Studies, and community video editing needs. We believe video production services play a crucial role in enhancing a university's communication, outreach, and educational efforts in several ways:

Student recruitment and marketing. To attract prospective students, universities use videos to showcase their campus, facilities, faculty, and student life. These videos provide an immersive experience that helps students envision themselves on campus, leading to increased enrollment.

Virtual campus tours. Especially important during times of restricted physical access, virtual tours through video allow potential students to explore the campus remotely. This is vital for international or distant students who may not have the means to visit in person.

Enhanced learning experience. Video content aids in delivering educational material more effectively. Lectures, tutorials, and demonstrations can be recorded and shared online, providing students with flexible learning opportunities to revisit at their own pace.

Engagement and retention. Engaging videos can increase student engagement. Whether it's informative content, event highlights, or testimonials, videos capture attention and can create a stronger connection with the university community, leading to higher student retention rates.

Alumni engagement and fundraising. Universities use videos to engage alumni by showcasing achievements, sharing success stories, and promoting fundraising campaigns. Compelling videos can evoke a sense of nostalgia and pride, encouraging former students to support their alma mater financially.

Research and knowledge dissemination. Videos are used to disseminate research findings, presentations, conferences, and seminars. They help reach a wider audience beyond academia, contributing to knowledge sharing and societal impact.

Brand building and reputation management. High-quality videos contribute significantly to a university's brand image. They can communicate the institution's values, achievements, and unique offerings, positively impacting its reputation both locally and globally.

Diversity and inclusion initiatives. Videos can be powerful tools to showcase the diversity within the university community, fostering an inclusive environment. Highlighting diverse perspectives, cultures, and achievements helps create a welcoming atmosphere for all.

Public relations and communication. Videos effectively communicate important announcements, updates, and messages from university leadership to students, faculty, staff, and the public.

Collaboration and partnerships. Universities often collaborate with various organizations, both within and outside academia. Videos can facilitate communication and collaboration by showcasing joint initiatives, partnerships, and shared achievements.

Chapter 13

Professional Development For Teachers

The longer I serve in academia, the more convinced I am that innovation is the key element to ensuring a prosperous future for academic institutions and the students we serve.

The question I come back to repeatedly is: Are our institutions of higher learning adequately preparing the next generation with workforce-readiness skills and the ability to innovate? If you didn't get the memo, industry is already taking the lead on this effort; they can't afford to wait.

Just like industry, higher education institutions must differentiate themselves from others in an ever-changing and competitive market. So why are some institutions consistently good at innovating and/or adapting while others seem to be blindsided by change? Is it because of their disciplined innovation process or the knowledge and skills of their faculty and staff? Or is it their determination to build a culture where challenging assumptions is not only encouraged, but expected?

In an overcrowded higher education market, institutions must focus on teaching creativity and innovation to attract high-caliber students, enable graduates to transition into quality careers with a competitive skill-set edge and differentiate themselves.

In one study, the Conference Board found that American employers think creativity and innovation are becoming increasingly important in the workforce and rate finding new hires with these skills to be among the most significant challenges facing CEOs.[52] Industry is not waiting for research to emerge from higher education; again, they can't wait.

Leading-edge organizations can only succeed in today's marketplaces and stoke innovation within their business models, products, and services with employees who are creative leaders.[53]

Innovation and creativity are at the leading edge of American businesses' most significant successes over the past century. Apple, for example, took an MP3 player, injected artistry, and came out with the iPod, leading to the rebirth of the corporation and the creation of a new consumer culture. Artistry and imagination are at the core of allowing technology to transcend the status of "product."

This creativity, artistry, and passion are evident in higher education classrooms nationwide. Students experiment in new fields, hone their craft over countless hours, and test and retest their ideas to integrate into their fields fully. These students are taking technologies and injecting the necessary ingredients to breed innovation.

Like the interplay of the right and left brain, industry is embracing the linkage between creative divergent thinking and convergent linear thinking in the workplace. IBM found in a recent study that "innovation has often been thought of as synonymous with invention—technicians in white coats working in labs producing new and unusual outcomes. However, innovation is not invention—it is conceptually much broader."[54] In their findings, innovation that does not add value is generally futile.

Industry continues to evolve and build on the innovative approach embraced by Apple and IBM. Higher education would be well served to evolve with this mindset as well. Further research and discussion about innovation are needed, but insufficient progress in developing innovation training in organizations worldwide exists. This is an opportunity for higher education and, specifically, continuing-education, professionals to meet this demand.

Chapter 14

Guests For College Credit

When Gabriella Salas first read the course description for "Ethnic Studies: Land And Labor," she was unsure what to expect. As a student at Hoover High School in San Diego, she had never taken a college-level class, but she took the leap and signed up.[55]

The course was one of three offered as part of the new Discover UC San Diego program, designed to give direct access to courses delivered by the university's world-renowned faculty. Beyond learning a new subject, students gain insights that may help them choose a major when applying to college, and the credits earned are transferable to any university accepting UC San Diego credits, helping them earn a degree faster.

"I didn't know what I was doing, I didn't have any time management skills, and I wasn't even confident in the work that I had turned in," explained Salas during the program's summer celebration. "By the end of this course…I learned how to not always doubt myself, how to properly manage my time, and I had gained a broader perspective of the world and other communities outside of my own."

The idea was sparked by several campus partners—including the Office for Educational Innovation, UC San Diego Division of Extended Studies, and the Teaching + Learning Commons. Recognizing that not every high school in San Diego offers students the chance to take honors courses—which would enable them to get a head start once enrolled in college—the team developed a new resource that could change a student's trajectory. This initiative is just one example of the university's collective impact approach, where multiple experts come together to execute a shared vision and accelerate impact.

In the summer of 2023, more than 120 students from the San Diego Unified School District enrolled in one of three courses offered in the pilot: "The Atmosphere," "Intro To Computer Science," and "Ethnic Studies: Land And Labor." Each class was uniquely developed to be accessible to high school students while maintaining the rigors of a college course that undergraduates would enroll in. Taught by UC San Diego faculty, students could explore a field of study they might like to pursue in college while previewing what it takes to complete a college course successfully.

At an event to celebrate the inaugural Discover UC San Diego cohort, three high school participants spoke about what they enjoyed most about the online course they enrolled in. Gabriella Salas gained self-confidence and time management skills; Vincent Nguyen could refine his work ethic and get a glimpse of college rigors; and Kimmy Dang was inspired by a topic she would never have pursued before.

For Crawford High School (San Diego) student Dang, enrolling in "The Atmosphere" opened a whole new way of seeing the world. "I learned about clouds and aerosols, balancing terrestrial and solar radiation, precipitation—topics that I could not have imagined touching upon in my high school education," she shared at the closing ceremony. "Everything was a surprise, and they all led to a greater appreciation of earth and its beauty. Trust me when I say in all the best ways, I will never look at a cloud the same way again."

UC San Diego professors equally relished the experience. "I really enjoyed the energy, insight, and creativity that the students of San Diego brought to the course," shared Lynn Russell, professor of atmospheric chemistry at Scripps Institution of Oceanography, who taught "The Atmosphere." "Many students told me how much they appreciated learning about the 'real' environment and the practical applications of the physics, chemistry, and math they had learned in school. They liked learning about how the atmosphere affects many aspects of life and how human activities affect the atmosphere."

What's next? New cohorts of high school students will continue to enroll in courses, with more options including American Sign Language. Course offerings will continue to grow, and instructional leaders plan to translate content into Spanish. The ultimate goal is to scale the program to extend across San Diego County and Imperial Valley, improving educational equity for more students.

Confidence building was at the heart of the program; hundreds of incoming UC San Diego students participate annually in Summer Bridge, a longstanding transition program that has become a beloved tradition.

Co-led by UC San Diego's Office of Academic Support and Instructional Services and the Teaching + Learning Commons, the program inspires fervent loyalty among participants, many of whom choose to return as mentors or staff members after graduating—like Martha Montoya Celedonio, a program alumna who is now a Summer Bridge staff member.

"Coming here was a big culture shock; it was a big thing to be the first person to go to college," said Montoya Celedonio, "As an English language learner, the writing hub helped me a lot, and being able to take courses early allowed me to mentally prepare and know what to expect. I'm very grateful for the experience."

Over the past forty-five years, the program has served thousands of first-generation and historically underserved students. One of the newest is Marie-Joe Franci, a first-year pharmacological chemistry student who moved to the US in 2020 from Beirut, Lebanon. She first attended Grossmont High School in El Cajon, California, then transferred to The Preuss School, a charter school on the UC San Diego campus, for her senior year. She chose to enroll at UC San Diego, drawn to the university for the opportunity to do undergraduate research.

After taking part in the five-week Summer Bridge program, Franci had two realizations: "First, it's important to stop procrastinating; Summer Bridge courses are fast paced so once you fall behind it's hard to catch up. Second, I learned that asking questions is important. You cannot expect to receive answers without asking. Summer Bridge staff can give you a lot of information, but all you have to do is ask."

Most of all, Franci feels more prepared to start her fall quarter. "Summer Bridge is a perfect program for students who are worried about getting lost in college," said Franci. "I've received a lot of support and guidance from a lot of mentors, and this makes me feel more confident about college life."

Like a rehearsal, Summer Bridge offers a glimpse of college life before the full premiere begins. Students can earn up to eight units of college credit while making friends, discovering resources, and finding belonging within the UC San Diego community. And it doesn't stop there; though the program kicks off in the summer, students benefit from peer mentorship, academic support, and social events throughout their entire first year.

Innovations That Were Created

These strategies have proven effective over decades. But the program continues to evolve to meet student needs. Here are just a few innovations that have happened:

RAFT week. As an orientation for Summer Bridge, the Teaching + Learning Commons launched RAFT Week, which stands for "Readjust, Acclimate, Familiarize, and Transform." This weeklong series helps students hone time management, communication, and study skills so they can begin to build their success toolbox.

Serving those with marginalized backgrounds. The Commons also prepares instructors to best serve students from marginalized backgrounds. This can look like creating a more inclusive syllabus and better understanding the responsibilities students undertake—for instance working multiple jobs in the summer as income providers for their families.

Math prep for STEM. A new math pilot program combines two introductory math classes to enable students to progress quickly enough to reach the foundational calculus course required for many STEM majors. The new course relies heavily on community-based support, with supplemental instruction sessions held by student peers.

Building a bridge. Summer Bridge has grown exponentially with the addition of virtual participation following the pandemic. Engagement went from 300 to over 700 students, with 75 percent enrolled virtually. Remote students living in the San Diego area are invited to the campus to participate in social activities, with transportation provided if necessary. Virtual options are also offered for those who can only take part online.

A Discovery Pathway For High School

When most of us think about college credit for high school students, Advanced Placement (AP) courses are top of mind. But research has found that AP success often does not translate to success in a major. Our professors find that sometimes AP is not the preparation for their coursework that students and parents assume that it is.

That's why we developed a discovery pathway for high school, community college, and adult/nontraditional students to get a taste of a specific discipline, gain college credit in the process, and incur little or no cost.

We want a pathway not just of access, not just dual enrollment, but providing support service. With this more student-centered approach we are not getting students ready for us, we are getting ready for them.

Traditionally, most continuing education programs do open enrollment or current enrollment; what we have done is open it up wide. We began in San Diego, then provided access to the Imperial Valley. At this point, we've expanded throughout the state of California and beyond. With this coursework available, students will be ready on day one when they choose UC San Diego or another college. We are building confidence in these students who are testing the waters and cutting down the time to graduation, which is a significant financial savings to the student.

Access Is Everything

Through this program, we're providing access to those who did not have it. Not everyone is invited into an AP course. AP is great, but the quality of instruction can vary from school to school, so having coursework that already meets our academic standards is helpful.

Our first proof of concept partner was San Diego Unified School District Superintendent Lamont Jackson. We appreciate the trust built with the school district, and the results speak for themselves. In the first year, we had well over 150 students in the first cohort.

What this does is prime the pipeline for access to students, whether they come to UC San Diego or not.

What students get is not a watered-down curriculum. This is taught by faculty and it's the same lower division course that you would take as a freshman at UC San Diego. This is a big deal because it's not just the typical concurrent model where you are a visitor and you have to go in person and blend in on your own, essentially with other students who are matriculated.

Step Two

The first step of this pilot was to offer the courses. Step two was to add courses focused on college preparation.

There must be more to the process than offering coursework and hoping for the best. We set up this program to help avoid "trip hazards" faced by many first-year students. Subjects would include, for instance, study skills, time management, and a variety of activities to get students acclimated to life (online or otherwise) at UC San Diego.

The program provides the holistic support needed so families, the parents, and the students, have those elements so that they not only take the course but are supported in that process. This student-centered approach is about the whole family experience, helping the student build confidence and a sense of belonging.

I remember interviewing someone for an outreach position, and they said, "my experience is that I am the person that is the bridge between access and success." That is what we are trying to do with this program—to be that bridge between access and success.

The Upshot

What is exciting about this program is that we are redefining how students discover and prepare for majors. Providing the ability to test the waters in this way, with support and encouragement along with the academic rigor of coursework, is removing barriers to on-time graduation and student satisfaction.

Beyond helping accelerate time to degree for students, we can help each academic program recruit students on their own terms, defining their own value proposition. Several other outcomes we had planned for are also coming to fruition as we help oversubscribed programs get students past bottleneck courses and reduce overcrowding.

With something more than AP courses available, we are leveling the resource and access playing field across school districts, adding new options for underserved learners in rural and other communities.

Chapter 15

Parent University

How can parents become more meaningfully involved in helping their children make decisions around college? How could institutions help connect with adults around lifelong learning for themselves and their children? At UC San Diego, we're doing it through a program called Parent and Caregiver Education (PACE)—aka Parent University.

Research and best practices suggest meaningful discussions about education require those involved to speak a common language, albeit in different dialects. In appreciation of this precept, the Education and Community Outreach program of UC San Diego's Division of Extended Studies offers contextually grounded programming for parents and caregivers under the auspices of PACE. Programming is delivered in English and Spanish without charge to schools, districts, and community-based organizations.

PACE workshops are custom-designed to attend to the unique needs of audiences in terms of content and delivery (face-to-face, blended/hybrid, and completely online). Each session is about an hour in duration and can be differentiated by age level (prekindergarten, elementary, secondary, and postsecondary) or tailored to meet the needs of multiage groups.

Workshops are augmented by short-form videos available for download from the Education Channel at UCTV and companion guides that may be found at the University of California Professional Development Institute. These resources are also publicly available without cost.

PACE sessions include the following:

- STEAM For Pre-K And Kindergarten
- STEAM For Elementary Students And Parents
- STEAM For Middle/High School Students And Parents
- Creating An Effective Environment For Learning At Home
- Brain-Compatible Learning For Parents
- Social And Emotional Needs And Stress Reduction
- Working With Teachers And School Communities: Models For Communication
- Finding "Flow" (Creativity, Persistence, And Resilience)
- Head, Heart, And Hands: Learning In And Through The Arts
- Understanding Next Generation Science Standards
- Understanding Common Core State Standards
- Learning Technologies And Remote Learning
- Adolescent Brain And Behavior
- Brave New Worlds: The Brain, Social Media, And Gaming
- Holistic Learning (Across Grade Levels)

- Effective Preparation For College And Career
- Supporting Literacy Development And Writing Effectiveness
- Understanding Giftedness, Talent, And Dual Exceptionality
- Supporting Essential Skills For The Twenty-First Century
- Demystifying The College Admissions Process

It is important to educate parents in preparing their children for college for several reasons:

Increased academic success. Parents who are informed and engaged in their children's education are more likely to provide support and resources that can lead to increased academic success, including better study habits, time management skills, and access to educational resources.

Improved college readiness. Preparing children for college requires a long-term strategy that includes academic preparation, financial planning, and social and emotional support. Educating parents about these topics can help them better support their children's college readiness and ensure that their children are prepared to succeed in college.

Financial planning. College can be expensive; many families may need to plan and save for years to afford tuition and other costs. Educating parents about financial planning and resources, such as scholarships and financial aid, can help ensure their children have the resources they need to pursue higher education.

Increased awareness of college options. Many families may not be aware of the variety of college options available, including community colleges, vocational schools, and online programs.

Educating parents about these options can help ensure that their children are aware of all the possibilities and can choose a college that best fits their needs and goals.

Overall, educating parents about preparing their children for college can help ensure that their children are academically and financially prepared for higher education and can increase their chances of success. Parent University can provide a valuable resource for parents by providing them with the knowledge and resources they need to support their children's college readiness.

Chapter 16

Mexico And Latin America

Having a campus that is not much more than a stone's throw away from the Mexican border brings an array of opportunities for connection and collaboration. Latinx/Chicanx culture is already a natural part of who we are as a San Diego-based institution, so developing deeper ties with Mexico and Latin American countries is an essential part of our mission and vision.

Being And Becoming A Hispanic-Serving Institution (HSI)

Nearly 25 percent of our undergraduate student enrollment comprises full-time Latinx students. When we reach that 25 percent goal, we will be eligible for HSI designation by the US Department of Education.

With so many US-based students to serve, why is it important to connect with Mexico and other Latin American countries? Besides the idea of being good neighbors, there are many compelling reasons for an institution of higher learning, specifically, its extension program, to forge these relationships.

The UC San Diego Division of Extended Studies has engaged in clinical trials education for nearly twenty years and has offered

Spanish courses for the last six years. "More and more, companies are pursuing clinical research in Latin America, both to control costs and to recruit more diverse patient populations. We are excited to expand the professional education available in Mexico and to contribute to the rising standard of clinical research being conducted globally," said program director Leonel Villa-Caballero, MD, PhD.

"A good foundation in clinical trials management will enable practitioners to optimally incorporate scientific advances and state-of-the-art health technologies," said Dr. Lucila Castro-Pastrana, a professor at UDLAP. Castro-Pastrana says the market for clinical studies is extremely competitive in Latin America and that the training is critical. The partnership also comes at a time when UDLAP is improving its research realm and adding a PhD program in molecular biomedicine, among other strategic initiatives.

The program will offer UDLAP students clinical trials courses online and in Spanish—at an affordable rate and via a Mexican invoice, which many employers require for tuition reimbursement. Candidates can also obtain grants and make payment plan arrangements through UDLAP. Students graduate with a diploma from UDLAP and with a Clinical Trials Administration certificate from UC San Diego, offering them the prestige of both organizations.

Both Drs. Villa-Caballero and Castro-Pastrana hope the forging of the partnership is just the first step in the relationship. "We hope eventually to have our instructors teach courses alongside UC San Diego's," said Castro-Pastrana, citing a "new bridge" between scholars and students across the Americas.

Mi Universidad

Mi Universidad is a program at UC San Diego that aims to support the success of Latinx students at the university. The program provides academic, social, and emotional support to students, with the goal of increasing retention and graduation rates among Latinx students.

Enrolling in classes exclusively for Spanish speakers offers the rare opportunity to find a community while building new, applicable skills. Margarita Coronel, a mother of three and a student at Mi Universidad, published an op-ed piece in the *San Diego Union-Tribune* titled "Local courses taught in Spanish are helping me—and my 10-year-old—develop job skills."[56]

As Morgan Appel, assistant dean for the Department of Education for the UC San Diego Division of Extended Studies, puts it, "To build a regional talent pipeline that truly catapults us to the top of the world, our universities need to think like entrepreneurs, building connections and capabilities." Appel has published on how universities would benefit from an entrepreneurial approach to education.[57]

Mi Universidad offers a variety of services and programs, including:

Academic support. Mi Universidad provides tutoring, academic coaching, and other resources to help students succeed academically. The program also offers academic workshops and study groups to help students develop effective study habits and improve their class performance.

Mentoring. Mi Universidad pairs students with mentors who provide guidance and support throughout their time at UC

San Diego. Mentors can help students navigate academic and personal challenges, connect with campus resources, and develop leadership skills.

Cultural events. Mi Universidad hosts a variety of cultural events and activities, including dances, film screenings, and guest lectures. These events provide opportunities for students to connect culturally and build community with other Latinx students on campus.

Career development. Mi Universidad offers workshops and resources to help students explore career options, build professional skills, and connect with potential employers.

Centro Fox. One of the many exciting initiatives happening at UC San Diego is an education exchange program coordinated with former president of Mexico Vicente Fox.

Through the program, high school students from the United States are invited to Centro Fox, a center for arts, leadership, and civic education at Fox's presidential library and complex in Guanajuato, Mexico, to attend presentations explaining the region's history, economy, and population. The program's overall goal is to encourage a population that consists largely of potential first-generation university students to continue their education beyond high school.

The program has already inspired connections with Mi Universidad. Program Director Nara Muniz I. França shares the story of one participant in the Centro Fox program that she was especially impressed by Mi Universidad.

"One of the kids from the program realized that his friends in his neighborhood were getting involved with drugs," says França.

"He lost a friend to an overdose, and another was mixed up with trafficking illegal drugs. He also noticed that all the kids liked hip-hop. He got a place that someone lent him where kids could go every day to mix and write hip-hop songs. They wrote the songs, practiced, and rehearsed it, and then someone would come and record it. But the condition of this project was that they could not use drugs. The seventeen-year-old boy managed this project by himself. He had the idea. He managed and implemented it. So, these are the kinds of projects they do."

Overall, Mi Universidad is an important program that provides critical support to Latinx students at UC San Diego. By providing academic, social, and emotional support, the program helps students succeed academically and personally and helps build a strong and supportive community on campus.

Chapter 17

Overcoming Stop-Outs

Every year, thousands of students leave universities without completing their degree. Finding these people and encouraging them to resume their education is an excellent way for campuses to boost enrollment and for lifelong learners to gain the skills and accreditation needed to fulfill their dreams and advance in their careers.

The Evolution Of Extension

My UC San Diego colleagues, Elizabeth H. Simmons and Hugo Villar, recently wrote, "…our traditional Extension model was limiting our ability to leverage these capabilities. On the one hand, Extension's work with nonmatriculated students was perceived as setting it apart from the university's core academic mission rather than enriching its multigenerational, multicultural reach. Extension's strengths were not well understood within the university, nor were the potential benefits of collaboration with Extension appreciated. Consequently, there was no deep intellectual connection with the academic schools and departments."[58]

The Extension Program and traditional academic programs had not been sharing data. The University had been missing opportunities. We had wanted to change that.

To that end, a working group was formed that has made the following accomplishments over the past five years:

- We reshaped the University Extension into the Division of Extended Studies. Among many benefits, this made the extension's mission more visible throughout the university community.

- We pulled the Division of Extended Studies into the university IT infrastructure, with students getting a more seamless experience moving from one program to the next.

- The Division of Extended Studies was integrated more fully into the university budgeting process, providing more transparency and tying more directly into the strategic planning processes of the university.

Stopping Stop-Outs

As UC San Diego Division of Extended Studies became more integral and less of an "add-on," we could focus on how to reach those students who have left UC San Diego without matriculating.

Like any other state university system, the entire University of California system wants to continue increasing enrollment. How can we do that? One excellent resource is people who have previously been a part of the community, whether in Los Angeles; Irvine, California; Davis, California; San Diego; or wherever.

Letting people know we can be a resource for degree completion or to take a few courses that will fulfill a career goal would go a long way in helping those students and growing our enrollment.

In a fall 2021 survey of more than 1,000 UC stop-outs, UC San Diego Center for Research + Evaluation researchers, under the direction of the University of California Office of the President, found that many former students expressed interest in completing a degree or certificate. Financial aid and course flexibility were key factors many noted that would make the process more feasible.[59]

In an article from *Inside Higher Ed*, researcher Patricia Steele is quoted as saying, "It's so clear that the barrier for students is institutions themselves, and that's not exclusive to adults. It's hard to transfer. It's hard to reenroll. It's hard to get credit for past experience or prior learning outside of school."[60]

The post-pandemic world has shown us how barriers, especially barriers of time and distance, can be managed by online learning options. But how else can institutions stop being barriers in and of themselves?

At UC San Diego we are working at eliminating barriers by reaching out to stop-outs and helping them to reenroll in programs that make sense for them now. There are any number of reasons to leave a program one has enrolled in. Family finances change. Goals and priorities change. If we can stay in touch and understand what formerly enrolled students need now that may be similar to or completely different from what originally brought them to UC San Diego, we absolutely want to be a part of that.

To stay connected to these needs, as the dean of Extended Studies, I now participate with the dean of undergraduate and graduate education on the council of academic deans and the senior team of administrative leaders. We are working together to clarify that extended studies have a key role and that together, we can serve learners of any age.

Chapter 18

Enhancing Campus Objectives

Writing in the *Harvard Business Review*, Marc Zao-Sanders says, "Lifelong learning is now roundly considered to be an economic imperative and 'the only sustainable competitive advantage.' Job candidates and employees who consider, update, and improve their skills are the high performers, especially over the longer term."[61]

Continuing education programs can be an effective tool for universities to be a major part of the lifelong learning plan of the people we serve.

By enhancing our core objectives, continuing education can assist universities in achieving their outreach goals and make lifelong learning as accessible as possible:

Reaching new audiences. Continuing education programs can attract students who may not have considered traditional degree programs or who are looking to enhance their skills and knowledge in a specific area. These programs can be marketed to nontraditional students, such as working professionals or individuals seeking to switch careers.

Diversifying revenue streams. Continuing education programs can generate revenue for universities and help them diversify their funding sources. These programs can be designed to be self-sustaining or profitable, which can help support the university's core mission and academic programs.

Strengthening community partnerships. Continuing education programs can provide opportunities for universities to partner with local businesses and organizations. These partnerships can lead to collaborations on research projects, internships, and other educational opportunities that benefit the community.

Fostering lifelong learning. Continuing education programs can help promote the idea of lifelong learning, which is becoming increasingly important in today's fast-paced and rapidly changing workplace. By providing opportunities for individuals to continue their education and professional development, universities can help ensure that alumni remain competitive in the job market and continue contributing to their communities.

Overall, continuing education programs can be an asset for universities looking to expand their reach and engage with new audiences. By designing innovative and relevant programs that meet the needs of students and the community, universities can enhance their impact and reputation while supporting their core mission of education and research.

Acknowledgments

Writing a book is never a solitary endeavor; it requires the support, encouragement, and contributions of many individuals. I extend my deepest gratitude to all those who have contributed to bringing this work to fruition.

First and foremost, I want to express my appreciation to Mary Walshok, Bruce Dunn, Judah Rosenwald, Shaul Kuper, and Morgan Appel, whose pioneering insights and unwavering dedication to lifelong learning have inspired not only the content of this book but also its very conception. Your passion for education and commitment to empowering learners of all ages have left an indelible mark on these pages.

I am profoundly grateful to my family, friends, staff, and colleagues who have offered invaluable feedback, encouragement, and support. Your insights and perspectives have enriched this work immeasurably, and I am fortunate to have had your guidance and camaraderie.

I extend my heartfelt thanks to my editor and publisher, Henry DeVries of Indie Books International, whose expertise, professionalism, and enthusiasm have helped shape this book into its final form. I am grateful for the opportunity to collaborate with you on this endeavor.

Finally, I offer my sincerest thanks to the readers who will embark on this journey of reinventing lifelong learning. I hope the ideas and insights in these pages will inspire you to embrace the transformative power of education and embark on your own path of lifelong learning.

With deepest appreciation,
Edward L. Abeyta, PhD

About the Author

Edward L. Abeyta, PhD serves as the Associate Dean for Education and Community Outreach at UC San Diego Division of Extended Studies, specializing in learning across the lifespan and the linkage among education, workforce development, and diverse communities across the globe.

Serving learners from precollege to retirement, Abeyta has dedicated his life to transforming education and empowering individuals to reach their full potential. With an unwavering commitment to innovation and access, he has made significant contributions to the academic community as an educator, author, public speaker, administrator, and advocate.

His commitment to empowering others extends beyond the classroom and administrative office. Abeyta is an education innovator who actively participates in binational community initiatives to create opportunities for underserved populations. His dedication to philanthropy has led him to support organizations focused on access, education, mentorship, and economic mobility, further solidifying his role as a catalyst for positive change.

Abeyta has been recognized by UC San Diego, the UC Office of the President, and the California Office of the Governor for his involvement in staff diversity and development initiatives and as a leader in donor stewardship. He serves on various community advisory boards and is a founding trustee of Urban Discovery Schools in San Diego, where he currently serves as the president of the UDA Foundation.

He has a BA from the University of New Mexico, an MA from the University of San Diego, and a PhD in Postsecondary Adult Education from Capella University. He served as the Staff Advisor to the University of California Regents from 2008–2010.

Works Cited And Author's Notes

[1] Edward Abeyta, "Value of Degrees Could Decline as Numbers Climb," *EvoLLLution*, November 20, 2013, https://evolllution.com/opinions/degrees-decline-numbers-climb.

[2] Edward Abeyta, "Lifelong Learning Starts Before Adulthood," *EvoLLLution*, December 3, 2012, https://evolllution.com/opinions/lifelong-learning-starts-before-adulthood/.

[3] Edward Abeyta, "Pre-Collegiate Program Pipeline Leaks: A Model of Inefficiency," *EvoLLLution*, October 6, 2014, https://evolllution.com/opinions/pre-collegiate-program-pipeline-leaks-model-inefficiency.

[4] Edward Abeyta, "Innovation Instruction Critical for Higher Education Institutions," *EvoLLLution*, June 10, 2013, https://evolllution.com/programming/program_planning/innovation-instruction-critical-higher-education-institutions.

[5] Paul F. Grendler, "The Universities of the Renaissance and Reformation," *Renaissance Quarterly* 57, no. 1 (Spring 2004), https://www.cambridge.org/core/journals/renaissance-quarterly/article/abs/universities-of-the-renaissance-and-reformation/9D9081CFBA90663F3727DE01F550D182.

⁶ Roger L. Geiger, *The History of American Higher Education: Learning and Culture from the Founding to World War II*, (Princeton, NJ: Princeton University Press, 2015) and Roger L. Geiger, *American Higher Education since World War II: A History*, (Princeton, NJ: Princeton University Press, 2019).

⁷ Geiger, *American Higher Education since World War II*.

⁸ "US Education Market Size, Share Global Analysis Report 2022-2030, Facts and Factors, February 2023, https://www.fnfresearch.com/us-education-market#:~:text=%5B214%2B%20Pages%20Report%5D%20According%20to%20the%20report%20published,%28CAGR%29%20of%20roughly%204.21%25%20between%202022%20and%202030.

⁹ "What America Needs to Know about Higher Education Redesign," Gallup, 2014, p. 10 and p. 25, https://www.gallup.com/file/services/176759/2013%20Gallup-Lumina%20Foundation%20Report.pdf.

¹⁰ Scott Jaschik and Doug Lederman, "The 2014 Inside Higher Ed Survey of College & University Chief Academic Officers," conducted by Gallup (Washington, DC: Inside Higher Ed, 2014), p. 13, https://www.insidehighered.com/sites/default/files/media/IHE_ProvostsSurvey-final.pdf.

¹¹ Jaimie Francis and Zac Auter, "3 Ways to Realign Higher Education with Today's Workforce," *Gallup Blog*, accessed January 19, 2024, http://www.gallup.com/education/231740/ways-realign-higher-education-today-workforce.aspx.

¹² John Hagel III, "What Motivates Lifelong Learners," *Harvard Business Review*, October 11, 2021, https://hbr.org/2021/10/what-motivates-lifelong-learners.

¹³ "UC San Diego Competencies," UC San Diego (website), accessed January 19, 2024, http://elt.ucsd.edu/_files/ucsd-competencies.pdf.

¹⁴ Jeffrey Selingo, "Higher Education's Push Toward Lifelong Learning," *The Atlantic*, December 12, 2022, https://www.

theatlantic.com/education/archive/2018/03/the-third-education-revolution/556091/.

[15] Edward Abeyta, "Snapshot Talk," EvoLLLution Symposium on Higher Ed and the Workforce, at Stanford University, 2014 IACEE International Conference, June 24, 2104, 30:07, https://www.youtube.com/watch?v=3EKZxlETBAE.

[16] Ashley Finley, "How College Contributes to Workforce Success," American Association of Colleges and Universities, 2021, https://dgmg81phhvh63.cloudfront.net/content/user-photos/Research/PDFs/AACUEmployerReport2021.pdf.

[17] Colleen Flaherty, "What Employers Want," Inside Higher Ed, April 5, 2021, https://www.insidehighered.com/news/2021/04/06/aacu-survey-finds-employers-want-candidates-liberal-arts-skills-cite-preparedness.

[18] Finley, "How College Contributes," p. 1.

[19] https://www.history.com/topics/renaissance/leonardo-da-vinci

[20] David Ching, "What is a land-grant university?" *The Persistent Pursuit* newsletter, Purdue University, March 23, 2023, https://stories.purdue.edu/what-is-a-land-grant-university

[21] Occupational Safety and Health (website), UC San Diego Extended Studies, accessed January 28, 2024, https://extendedstudies.ucsd.edu/osha/home.

[22] Ray would eventually retire in 2010.

[23] "Fast Facts: Educational Attainment," National Center for Education Statistics, https://nces.ed.gov/fastfacts/display.asp?id=27.

[24] Jennifer Ma and Matea Pender, "Education Pays 2023: The Benefits of Higher Education for Individuals and Society," College Board, 2023, https://research.collegeboard.org/media/pdf/education-pays-2023.pdf.

[25] Anthony P. Carnevale and Donna M. Desrochers, "Help Wanted… Credentials Required: Community Colleges in the Knowledge

Economy," Educational Testing Service, 2001, https://files.eric.ed.gov/fulltext/ED451832.pdf.

26. James Murphy, "A Degree of Waste: The Economic Benefits of Educational Expansion," *Oxford Review of Education* 19, no. 1 (1993): 9–31.

27. Alison Wolf, *Does Education Matter? Myths About Education and Economic Growth*, (London: Penguin Books, 2002).

28. "Occupational Employment and Wages, May 2022," US Bureau of Labor Statistics (website), last modified April 25, 2023, https://www.bls.gov/oes/current/oes172141.htm.

29. "Research Summary: Education and Lifetime Earnings," Research, Statistics, and Policy Analysis, Social Security Administration (website), November 2015, https://www.ssa.gov/policy/docs/research-summaries/education-earnings.html.

30. Florence Xiaotao Ran and Yuxin Lin, "Rethinking Remedial Programs to Promote College Student Success," Brookings Institution (website), February 15, 2022, https://www.brookings.edu/articles/rethinking-remedial-programs-to-promote-college-student-success/. Xianglei Chen et al., "Courses Taken, Credits Earned, and Time to Degree: A First Look at the Postsecondary Transcripts of 2011–12 Beginning Postsecondary Students" (NCES 2020-501). US Department of Education, Washington, DC: National Center for Education, April 2020, https://nces.ed.gov/pubsearch/pubsinfo.asp?pubid=2020501.

31. Deborah J. Cohan, "Why Undecided Is A Great College Major, *Psychology Today*, June 25, 2021. https://www.psychologytoday.com/us/blog/social-lights/202106/why-undecided-is-great-college-major

32. Edward Abeyta, "Work-Based Learning and Continuing Education: Connecting the K–12 Classroom to Real Life," *EvoLLLution*, May 20, 2013, http://evolllution.com/opinions/work-based-learning-continuing-education-connecting-k-12-classroom-real-life/.

[33] John Brennan and Brenda Little, "Towards a Strategy for Workplace Learning," Centre for Higher Education Research & Information, May 2006, http://oro.open.ac.uk/6437/1/towardsastrategyrd09_06.pdf.

[34] Christine D. Bremer and Svjetlana Madzar, "Encouraging Employer Involvement in Youth Apprenticeship and Other Work-Based Learning Experiences for High School Students," *Journal of Vocational and Technical Education* 12, no. 1 (Fall 1995), http://scholar.lib.vt.edu/ejournals/JVTE/v12n1/bremer.html.

[35] Abeyta, "Work-Based Learning."

[36] Patrick M. Callan, Peter T. Ewell, Joni E. Finney, and Dennis P. Jones, "Good Policy, Good Practice: Improving Outcomes and Productivity in Higher Education; A Guide for Policymakers," (San Jose, CA: National Center for Public Policy and Higher Education, November 2007), https://files.eric.ed.gov/fulltext/ED499122.pdf.

[37] Wendy Erisman and Shannon M. Looney, "Corporate Investments in College Readiness and Access," (Washington, DC: Institute for Higher Education Policy, June 2008), https://files.eric.ed.gov/fulltext/ED518025.pdf.

[38] Reaching for College, Vol. 1, *Directory of College-School Partnerships*, Vol. 2, Case Studies of College-School Partnerships (Rockville, MD: Westat, Inc., December 1992) https://files.eric.ed.gov/fulltext/ED356713.pdf and https://files.eric.ed.gov/fulltext/ED356714.pdf.

[39] Angela Alvarado Coleman. "The Effect of Pre-Collegiate Academic Outreach Programs on First-Year Financial Aid Attainment, Academic Achievement and Persistence." http://eric.ed.gov/?id=ED534673

[40] National Association for College Admission Counseling, (2004) Short term early college awareness: Key strategies for successful early intervention and early college awareness programs.

Alexandria, VA: National Association for College Admission Counseling.

41 "Increasing College Opportunity for Low-Income Students: Promising Models and a Call to Action," Executive Office of the President, White House (website), January 2014, https://obamawhitehouse.archives.gov/sites/default/files/docs/increasing_college_opportunity_for_low-income_students_report.pdf.

42 Nicole Spector, "How Much Does It Cost for College Test Preparation and Is It Worth It?" GOBankingRates (website), August 15, 2022, https://www.gobankingrates.com/saving-money/education/how-much-does-test-preparation-cost-is-it-worth-it/.

43 Matea Pender, Jonathan Smith, Michael Hurwitz, and Jessica Howell, "College Choice: Informing Students' Trade-Offs between Institutional Price and College Completion," College Board Advocacy and Policy Center, October 2012, p. 13, https://files.eric.ed.gov/fulltext/ED541968.pdf.

44 Swail, "Preparing America's Disadvantaged."

45 Jennifer McEntee, "New Marine Science Program Empowers Teens to Become Stewards of the Ocean," *UC San Diego Extended Studies Blog*, September 2, 2021, https://extendedstudies.ucsd.edu/news-and-events/division-of-extended-studies-blog/september-2021/new-marine-science-program-empowers-teens-to-becom.

46 Margaret King, "Students Share Co-Author Credit for Journal Article on ADHD Risk Factors," *UC San Diego Extended Studies Blog*, December 17, 2021, https://extendedstudies.ucsd.edu/news-and-events/division-of-extended-studies-blog/december-2021/students-share-co-author-credit-for-journal-articl.

47 "Turning the Dream of a College Education into a Reality," *UC San Diego Extended Studies Blog*, October 5, 2015, https://extendedstudies.ucsd.edu/news-and-events/division-of-extended-

studies-blog/october-2015/turning-the-dream-of-a-college-education-into-a-reality.

[48] Edward Abeyta, "New Ways to Bridge Gap from High School to College," *UC San Diego Extended Studies Blog,* February 29, 2012, https://extendedstudies.ucsd.edu/news-and-events/division-of-extended-studies-blog/february-2012/new-ways-to-bridge-gap-from-high-school-to-college.

[49] Jay Mathews, "America's Hottest Colleges," *Newsweek,* August 21, 2005, https://www.newsweek.com/americas-hot-colleges-117547.

[50] "CTE General Public Fact Sheet," California Department of Education (website), last reviewed September 27, 2022, https://www.cde.ca.gov/ci/ct/gi/ctegeneralfacts.asp.

[51] "Learning for a Lifetime," *UC San Diego Extended Studies Blog,* July 14, 2018, https://extendedstudies.ucsd.edu/news-and-events/division-of-extended-studies-blog/july-2018/learning-for-a-lifetime.

[52] "Innovation Begins with Creative Employees," Conference Board (website), June 22, 2010, http://www.conference-board.org/webcasts/ondemand/webcastdetail.cfm?webcastid=2245.

[53] Barbara J. Lombardo and Daniel John Roddy, "Cultivating Organizational Creativity in the Age of Complexity," IBM, 2011, https://www.creativityatwork.com/wp-content/uploads/2011/08/IBM-creative-leadershipstudy-2011.pdf.

[54] "Enterprise Innovation Accelerator: Creating Opportunities for Sustainable Growth through Innovation," IBM, 2012, http://ftpmirror.your.org/pub/misc/ftp.software.ibm.com/common/ssi/ecm/gb/en/gbs03133usen/GBS03133USEN.PDF.

[55] "Gaining College and College Credits," UC San Diego Today, Sept. 19, 2023, https://today.ucsd.edu/story/gaining-confidence-and-college-credits.

[56] Margarita Coronel, "Opinion: Local courses taught in Spanish are help me—and my 10-year-old—develop job skills," *San Diego Union-Tribune,* Feb. 9, 2024.

57 Morgan Appel, Opinion: Here's how universities would benefit from an 'entrepreneurial' approach to education," *San Diego Union-Tribune*, Feb. 9, 2024.

58 Elizabeth H. Simmons and Hugo Villar, "Evolving 'Extension,'" Views, Inside Higher Ed, July 21, 2023, https://www.insidehighered.com/opinion/views/2023/07/21/why-and-how-we-rethought-role-extension-opinion.

59 Kelly Nielsen, "California's Six Million Stop Outs: Getting from Some College to a College Degree," *UC San Diego Extended Studies Blog*, July 11, 2022, https://extendedstudies.ucsd.edu/news-and-events/division-of-extended-studies-blog/july-2022/california%E2%80%99s-six-million-stop-outs-getting-from-so.

60 Katherine Knott, "Bringing Back Stop Outs," Inside Higher Ed, August 22, 2022, https://www.insidehighered.com/news/2022/08/23/uc-program-seeks-re-enroll-adults-who-stopped-out.

61 Marc Zao-Sanders, "Identify—and Hire—Lifelong Learners," *Harvard Business Review*, May 13, 2021, https://hbr.org/2021/05/identify-and-hire-lifelong-learners.0000

Index

Academic Connections, 53–56
ACT, 43
ADHD, 48–49, 112
American Association of Colleges and Universities, 8, 11, 109
Auter, Zac, 6, 108

Barrio Logan College Institute, 51, 53
Biosphere 2, 54
Bishop's School, The, 48
Boz Life Science Research and Teaching Institute, 48
Bozinovic, Kesten, 49
Bradbury, Ray, 2

Co-Curricular Record (CCR), 9
College Board, 40–41, 43, 109, 112
Competencies, 6–10, 108
Council for the Advancement of Standards in Higher Education (CAS), 8
Cruz, José, 51

Darwin, Charles, 5
Experience design, 14, 17
Feng, Zuying, 49
Finley, Ashley, 11, 109
Francis, Jaimie, 6, 108

G.I. Bill, 3
Gallup poll, 6
Garcia, Guillermo, 53
Geiger, Roger, 3, 108
Grendler, Paul, 2, 107
Haagensen, Sora, 47–51
Hagel, John, 7, 108
Harvard Business Review, 7, 101, 108, 114
Inside Higher Ed, 6, 99, 108–109, 114
Los Alamos National Laboratory, 55
Lumina Foundation, 6
McLamb, Flannery, 49

Mi Universidad, 93–95
National Association of Colleges and Employers Career Readiness Competencies, 8
National College Access Program Directory, 41
O'Connell, Katherine (Katie), 47–50
Olander, Natalie, 47–50
Oregon Bioscience Association, 48
OSHA, 25–26, 109

Parton, Brent, 10

Ray, Ellen, 25
Renaissance, The, 1–5, 7, 9, 107, 109
Research Scholars Program, 45–47, 51

SAT, 43, 50–51
Scientific Reports, 49
STEAM, 14, 57–59, 88
Steele, Patricia, 99
STEM, 14, 83

UC San Diego, ix–x, 7, 9, 11, 22, 25, 40, 45–46, 48, 51, 53–58, 62–63, 67, 71–72, 79–87, 91–95, 97–99, 105–106, 108–109, 112–114
UC San Diego Center for Research and Evaluation, 99
UC San Diego Division of Extended Studies, 46, 48, 51, 53–54, 58, 62, 71–72, 80, 91, 93, 98, 105
US Education Market, 5, 108

WASC Senior College and University Commission Core Competencies, 8
White House, 42, 112
Widner, Leslie, 21–22
Wolf, Alison, 28, 110
World War II, 1, 3, 108

Yen, Nicole, 46

Zao-Sanders, Mark, 101, 114

www.ingramcontent.com/pod-product-compliance
Lightning Source LLC
Chambersburg PA
CBHW031634160426
43196CB00006B/412